Editor
Eric Migliaccio

Cover Artist
Marilyn Goldberg

Editor in Chief
Ina Massler Levin, M.A.

Creative Director
Karen J. Goldfluss, M.S. Ed.

Art Coordinator
Renée Christine Yates

Imaging
James Edward Grace
Craig Gunnell

Materials contained in this publication are copyrighted by Evans Newton Incorporated, 15941 N. 77th St., Suite 1, Scottsdale, AZ 85260.

www.evansnewton.com
© 2000-2008

Publisher
Mary D. Smith, M.S. Ed.

Developed and Written by
Evans Newton Incorporated

The classroom teacher may reproduce copies of materials in this book for classroom use only. Reproduction of any part for an entire school or school system is strictly prohibited. No part of this publication may be transmitted, stored, or recorded in any form without written permission from the publisher.

Teacher Created Resources, Inc.
6421 Industry Way
Westminster, CA 92683
www.teachercreated.com

ISBN: 978-1-4206-6221-4

© 2009 Teacher Created Resources, Inc.
Made in U.S.A.

Table of Contents

Introduction 3
Standards Correlation Chart 4
Reading and Writing Lessons
   Skill 1: Consonants and Vowels 6
   Skill 2: Phonemic Awareness 12
   Skill 3: Reading Basics 22
   Skill 4: Parts of a Book 27
   Skill 5: Letter Sounds 30
   Skill 6: Letter and Sound Sequence 34
   Skill 7: Rhymes and Repeated Sounds 39
   Skill 8: Meaning of Texts 44
   Skill 9: Colors, Numbers, and Shapes 49
   Skill 10: Naming Words and Action Words 52
   Skill 11: All About "I" 57
   Skill 12: Comparing Forms of Text 62
   Skill 13: Main Idea 65
   Skill 14: Summarizing Text 71
   Skill 15: Parts of a Story 75
   Skill 16: Illustrations 79
   Skill 17: Oral-Graphic Directions 83
   Skill 18: Making Predictions 89
   Skill 19: Asking Questions 94
   Skill 20: Fiction vs. Nonfiction 106
   Skill 21: Uppercase and Lowercase Letters 112
   Skill 22: Capitalization and Punctuation 143
   Skill 23: Sentence Patterns 147
   Skill 24: Using Graphic Organizers 153

PAL Packets
   Introduction 162
   Sample PAL Packet (English) 163
   Sample PAL Packet (Spanish) 170

Introduction

The *Essential Skills* series was developed in response to an overwhelming number of teachers frustrated by the fact that their students didn't have all of the skills needed to be taught the on-grade-level standards. Due to this dilemma, the staff at Evans Newton Incorporated reviewed the standards from the national organizations (NCTM, NCTE, IRA, etc.) and many states to determine the top prerequisite skills that a student going into a certain grade level should know to be successful in that grade. The skills represented here are a compilation of many different states' standards and do not represent any one state's requirements. Since the introduction of skills vary slightly in some states, you may find it useful to also review and select *Essential Skills* books for the grade higher and the grade lower than you are teaching in addition to your own grade level.

The *Essential Skills* lessons were designed using the theories of many leading educational theorists. It is easy to see the influence of Madeline Hunter's *Essential Elements of Effective Instruction* used in the "Recall," "Review," and "Wrap-up" sections. They were also designed using Grant Wiggins's Backwards Design Model, making sure the outcome and the assessment pieces were written before designing the actual instruction to go with them. In the questions included in the lesson, you will see many different levels from Bloom's Taxonomy represented, a reflection of the work of Benjamin Bloom.

As indicated before, the skills were written to cover skills taught at a previous grade level—generally just the preceding grade. *The Essential Skills* series was designed in a cumulative fashion—i.e., the skills from one grade level build on the skills from the previous grade level. If a student is multiple years behind, then going down to previous levels of the *Essential Skills* may be helpful. Please note that the lessons are meant to be review lessons that will help students activate prior knowledge. If students have never been taught the skill before, then the lessons will probably not be enough for the students to become proficient in the skill without further support.

Teachers from many different states and many different grade levels have found the *Essential Skills* to be very helpful at various times of the school year.

- ✸ Some teachers use the lessons at the beginning of the year to review important skills.
- ✸ Some teachers use the lessons throughout the year to introduce topics as they come up in their scope and sequence.
- ✸ Some teachers use the *Essential Skills* books for the next grade level following their state test as a way to prepare their students for the following school year.

In all of these situations, teachers have found the *Essential Skills* series to be helpful in building student's knowledge and preparing them to master the content that the states require students to know.

In addition to the classroom uses described above, books in the *Essential Skills* series have also proven to be effective tools for special programs such as after-school tutoring programs, summer-school programs, and Special Education programs where teachers need to solidify students' skills and help them progress towards excelling at on-grade-level content.

We truly hope that you enjoy using the *Essential Skills* books with your students and find them to be highly useful, as has been the case with the many teachers who have used them before you.

Standards Correlation Chart

Listed below are the McREL standards for Language Arts. All standards and benchmarks are used with permission from McREL.

Copyright 2006 McREL. Mid-continent Research for Education and Learning. Address: 2250 S. Parker Road, Suite 500, Aurora, CO 80014. Telephone: (303) 337-0990. Website: *www.mcrel.org/standards-benchmarks*.

Standards and Benchmarks	Skill # (Pages)
Standard 3. Uses grammatical and mechanical conventions in written compositions	
• **Benchmark 1.** Uses conventions of print in writing (e.g., forms letters in print, uses upper- and lowercase letters of the alphabet, spaces words and sentences, writes from left-to-right and top-to-bottom, includes margins)	Skill 1 (6-11); Skill 3 (22-26); Skill 21 (112-142)
• **Benchmark 3.** Uses nouns in written compositions	Skill 10 (52-56)
• **Benchmark 4.** Uses verbs in written compositions	Skill 10 (52-56)
• **Benchmark 7.** Uses conventions of spelling in written compositions (e.g., spells high frequency, commonly misspelled words from appropriate grade-level list; spells phonetically regular words; uses letter-sound relationships; spells basic short vowel, long vowel, r-controlled, and consonant blend patterns; uses a dictionary and other resources to spell words)	Skill 2 (12-21); Skill 5 (30-33); Skill 6 (34-38); Skill 7 (39-43)
• **Benchmark 8.** Uses conventions of capitalization in written compositions	Skill 22 (143-146)
• **Benchmark 9.** Uses conventions of punctuation in written compositions	Skill 22 (143-146); Skill 23 (147-152)
Standard 4. Gathers and uses information for research purposes	
• **Benchmark 2.** Uses a variety of sources to gather information	Skill 24 (153-161)

Standards Correlation Chart

Standards and Benchmarks	Skill # (Pages)
Standard 5. Uses the general skills and strategies of the reading process	
• **Benchmark 1.** Uses mental images based on pictures and print to aid in comprehension of text	Skill 16 (79-82); Skill 17 (83-88)
• **Benchmark 2.** Uses meaning clues to aid comprehension and make predictions about content	Skill 4 (27-29); Skill 8 (44-48); Skill 18 (89-93)
Standard 6. Uses reading skills and strategies to understand and interpret a variety of literary texts	
• **Benchmark 1.** Uses reading skills and strategies to understand a variety of familiar literary passages and texts	Skill 20 (106-111)
• **Benchmark 3.** Knows setting, main characters, main events, sequence, and problems in stories	Skill 15 (75-78)
• **Benchmark 4.** Knows the main ideas or theme of a story	Skill 13 (65-70)
Standard 7. Uses reading skills and strategies to understand and interpret a variety of informational texts	
• **Benchmark 1.** Uses reading skills and strategies to understand a variety of informational texts	Skill 12 (62-64)
• **Benchmark 2.** Understands the main idea and supporting details of simple expository information	Skill 19 (94-105)
• **Benchmark 3.** Summarizes information found in texts	Skill 12 (62-64)

Consonants and Vowels

Skill 1: The student will recognize consonants and vowels.

Instructional Preparation

Materials:

- classroom display of the alphabet

Duplicate the following (one per student, unless otherwise indicated):

- "Consonants and Vowels!" reference sheet
- "Which Is It?" handouts

Prepare a transparency of the following:

- "Consonants and Vowels!" reference sheet
- "Snack Time" story
- "Which Is It?" handouts

Recall

Before beginning the **Review** component, tell the students that you are going to ask them questions about the alphabet. Direct them to study the letters of the alphabet posted in the classroom. Facilitate a discussion based on the following questions:

* Which letters of the alphabet are consonants? (*b, c, d, f, g, h, j, k, l, m, n, p, q, r, s, t, v, w, x, z, and sometimes y*)
* Which letters of the alphabet are vowels? (*a, e, i, o, u, and sometimes y*)

Review

1. Distribute copies of the "Consonants and Vowels!" reference sheet and display the transparency. Read each section aloud while the students read along silently. Facilitate a discussion based on the following questions:

   * Which group has the most letters? (*consonants*)
   * How many letters are vowels? (*6*)
   * What is special about the letter *y*? (*A "y" is a consonant when it makes the sound as in "your," but "y" is a vowel when it makes a vowel sound as in "by."*)

Consonants and Vowels (cont.)

Review (cont.)

2. Write the name of your school and the headings "Consonants" and "Vowels" on the classroom board. Allow the students to refer to their reference sheet as you ask the following questions:

   * Which letters in the name of our school are consonants? (*Responses will vary; accept all reasonable responses.*)
   * Which letters in the name of our school are vowels? (*Responses will vary; accept all reasonable responses.*)

   Ask volunteers to come to the classroom board and write the responses under the appropriate headings. Guide the volunteers to the correct heading, if necessary. Use the responses to emphasize how to identify consonants and vowels.

	Consonants	Vowels
Pine	P n	i e
Avenue	v n	A e u e
School	S c h l	o o

3. Display the "Snack Time" story. Read the story aloud as the students read along silently. Discuss the story, pointing out that each word in the story is made up of letters and that each letter is either a consonant or a vowel.

4. Distribute copies of the "Which Is It?" handouts and display the transparency. Begin by having each student write his or her name on the appropriate line at the top of the page. Then explain to the students that they are going to play a letter game with the words in the displayed story. Point to the word *school* in the first paragraph. In the *Example* section on the handout, model identifying each of the letters in the word as a consonant or vowel and writing them in the appropriate column. Use other words in the story to guide the students through more examples as needed. Be sure to model a word such as *only*, in which the *y* functions as a vowel and a word such as *you*, in which the *y* functions as a consonant. When the students are ready, have them practice responding independently. Have each student complete the handouts by breaking five words into consonants and vowels. Have the students check their responses with a neighbor, then have them hold up the responses for your review. Discuss the responses for accuracy.

Wrap-Up

* To conclude this lesson, have the students respond orally to the following question: *How can you tell if a letter is a consonant or a vowel?*

* Discuss the students' responses for accuracy. Use their responses to review the letters that are consonants and the letters that are vowels.

Consonants and Vowels (cont.)

Reference Sheet

Each letter of the alphabet is a consonant or vowel.

Consonants

b c d f g h j k l m n p q r s t v w x (y) z

Vowels

a e i o u (y)

What is y?

The letter *y* is a consonant when it makes a sound as in these words:
your you yellow yam yo-yo

The letter *y* is a vowel when it makes a vowel sound as in these words:
by fly style stay monkey

Consonants and Vowels (cont.)

Snack Time

Jim came home after school. He walked into the kitchen. "May I have a cookie for a snack?" he asked his mom.

"Yes, Jim, you may," said Mom. "Eat only one," she added. Jim ate a cookie. Mom went out to the yard. He ate more.

Later, he had a tummy ache. His mom took care of him. "Mom?" said Jim.

"Yes," said Mom.

"I have something to tell you," he said. "I ate more than one cookie. I am sorry. Will you forgive me?"

"Yes," said Mom. "I just hope your tummy can, too!"

Name: _____

Consonants and Vowels *(cont.)*

Which Is It?

Example.

Word: _____school_____

Consonants	Vowels

1.

Word: _____

Consonants	Vowels

2.

Word: _____

Consonants	Vowels

Name: _____

Consonants and Vowels *(cont.)*

Which Is It? *(cont.)*

3.
Word: _____

Consonants	Vowels

4.
Word: _____

Consonants	Vowels

5.
Word: _____

Consonants	Vowels

Phonemic Awareness

Skill 2: The student will demonstrate phonemic awareness by blending or segmenting phonemes in one-syllable words.

Instructional Preparation

Duplicate the following (one per student, unless otherwise indicated):

- "Sounds: Vowels" reference sheet
- "Sounds: Consonants" reference sheet
- "Sounds: Digraphs" reference sheet
- "Sounds: Diphthongs and Blends" reference sheet
- "The Lost Book" handouts

Prepare a transparency of the following:

- "Sounds: Vowels" reference sheet
- "Sounds: Consonants" reference sheet
- "Sounds: Digraphs" reference sheet
- "Sounds: Diphthongs and Blends" reference sheet
- "The Lost Book" handouts

Recall

Before beginning the **Review** component, facilitate a discussion based on the following questions:

- ✳ What two types of letters are there in the alphabet? (*consonants and vowels*)
- ✳ What sound does a vowel—for example, *e*—make in a word? (*Accept appropriate responses.*)
- ✳ Does a vowel—for example, *e*—always make the same sound in a word?

Review

1. To begin the lesson, write on the classroom board the following words:

    made   paint   stay

    Read aloud each of the words while the students read them silently. Then read them aloud again, having the students echo read the words. Ask the following questions (below and on page 13):

    - ✳ What are the vowels in the word *made*? ("*a*" and "*e*")
    - ✳ Since the *e* is silent in the word *made*, what is the vowel sound you hear? (*the long /a/ sound*)

Phonemic Awareness *(cont.)*

Review *(cont.)*

* What are the vowels in the word *paint*? (*"a" and "i"*)
* What is the vowel sound you hear in the word *paint*? (*the long /a/ sound*)
* What are the vowels in the word *stay*? (*"a" and "y"*)
* What is the vowel sound you hear in the word *stay*? (*the long /a/ sound*)

Discuss how the vowel sound in each of the words is the same (*the long /a/ sound*), even though the vowel or combination of vowels is different in each word. Tell the students they need to understand the different sounds vowels or vowel combinations make in words. Ask volunteers to share other words they know that have the long /a/ sound. When discussing *y* as a vowel in the word *stay*, explain that the letter *y* is a consonant that is sometimes used as a vowel. It is used as a vowel in this case and also in the words *any, boy, buy, by, cry, day, fly, try, why*, etc. It is used as a consonant in the words *yard, year, your*, etc.

2. Write on the classroom board the following words:

    than   *thank*

Read aloud each word while the students read them silently. Then read them aloud again, having the students echo-read the words. Ask the following questions:

* What two consonants begin the word *than*? (*"t" and "h"*)
* What sound do these consonants make when you read the word *than*? (*Students should say the /th/ sound as it relates to the short /a/ sound in "than."*)
* What two consonants begin the word *thank*? (*"t" and "h"*)
* What sound do these consonants make when you read the word *thank*? (*Students should say the "hissing" /th/ sound as it relates to the short /a/ sound in "thank."*)

Discuss how the sound of the adjacent letters *th* is different in each word. Tell the students they need to understand the different sounds consonants and consonant combinations make in words. Ask volunteers to share other words they know of that have the different /th/ sounds, making a T-chart on the classroom board to show the different /th/ sounds in the words. Tell the students that in this lesson they will be learning/reviewing the different vowel and consonant sounds and the sounds that combinations of vowels and/or consonants can make to practice understanding and reading one-syllable words.

Th in "than"	Th in "thank"
that	think
they	thimble
this	thought

Phonemic Awareness *(cont.)*

Review *(cont.)*

3. Distribute copies of the "Sounds: Vowels" reference sheet and display the transparency. Read through the different short and long vowel sounds and the examples of each with the students, drawing their attention to the underlined vowel in each example. Ask volunteers to share words they know that exhibit the short and long vowel sounds shown on this page.

4. Next, distribute copies of the "Sounds: Consonants" reference sheet and display the transparency. Read through the consonant sounds and examples with the students, drawing their attention to the underlined consonant in each example and discussing the different sounds the letter *c* makes by using the two-syllable word *circus*, since this word demonstrates both of the sounds a *c* can make. Ask volunteers to share words they know that have the different consonant sounds. You may wish to write the shared words on a sheet of chart paper or the classroom board.

5. Distribute copies of the "Sounds: Digraphs" reference sheet and display the transparency. Read aloud the definition of vowel digraphs while the students read along silently. Read through the examples, highlighting the long vowel sound each exhibits. Explain that in vowel digraphs, it is usually the sound of the first vowel that is heard when the word is pronounced, while the second vowel is silent. To emphasize this point, tell the students that it is the first vowel that does the "talking." Allow volunteers to share additional words that contain vowel digraphs. You may wish to write these additional vowel digraphs on a sheet of chart paper or the classroom board. Have the students choral- or echo-read the words once all the additional words containing vowel digraphs have been shared and recorded. Repeat the process of reading the definition, discussing the examples, and sharing additional examples with consonant digraphs at the bottom of this reference sheet.

6. Distribute copies of the "Sounds: Diphthongs and Blends" reference sheet and display the transparency so that only the section on diphthongs is visible. Read aloud the definition of *diphthong* while the students read along silently. Read through the examples, explaining that when pronouncing a diphthong, we begin with a vowel sound and then move our mouths to another vowel or consonant sound within the same sound. Model for the students how your lips change position when you pronounce the diphthong "oy" in the words *boy* and *toy*. Allow volunteers to share additional words that contain diphthongs, record them, and have the class choral- or echo-read them, if applicable.

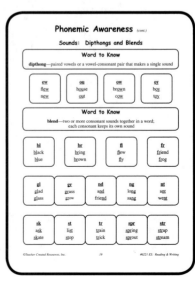

#6221 ES: Reading & Writing 14 ©Teacher Created Resources, Inc.

Phonemic Awareness *(cont.)*

Review *(cont.)*

7. Distribute copies of the first page of "The Lost Book" handouts and display the transparencies. Read the story aloud while the students read it silently. Pose the following prompt:

    * "Listen carefully as I read you a word from the story "The Lost Book" and then the sounds of that word. *Room. R–oo–m.* I am going to reread the first paragraph in the story and circle the word that says *room*."

    Explain that in the word *room*, each consonant and digraph is its own sound and that one-syllable words are separated or divided into sounds. Reread the first paragraph aloud while the students read along silently. Tell them that when they read the word *room* they should put a finger on the word and raise their hand. Once they have identified the correct word, circle the word *room* on the transparency and ask the students to do the same on their copy. Then have them write the word in one of the boxes below the passage after you demonstrate on the transparency.

8. Then pose the following prompt:

    * "Listen carefully as I read you a word from the story and then the sounds of that word. *Asked. A–sk–ed.* Reread the first paragraph of the story and circle the word that says *asked*."

    Give the students time to reread the first paragraph, identify the word *asked*, and circle it. Circulate throughout the room to make sure they are circling the correct word. Then have the students write the word *asked* in one of the boxes below the passage.

9. Direct the students' attention back to the first page of "The Lost Book" handout, and pose the following prompt:

    * "Listen carefully as I read you a word from the story and then the sounds of that word. *Where. Wh–ere.* Reread the story and circle the word that says *where*."

    Give the students time to reread the passage to identify the word *where* and circle it. Circulate throughout the room to make sure they are circling the correct word and to provide assistance when needed. Remind them to write the word *where* in one of the boxes below the passage. Continue using the format of this prompt with the words *first*, *wished*, and *must*. Make sure you review the circled and recorded words for accuracy. If additional practice is needed, you may use the above prompt to have the students identify additional words from the second page of the passage.

Wrap-Up

- To conclude instruction, have the students reread the first page of "The Lost Book" story to identify the words *last* and *would*. Give the students time to reread the passage and identify these words, then ask volunteers to come to the overhead, point out these words on the transparency, and circle them.

- Ask volunteers to share the sounds and type of sounds in each word that were blended or separated in order to identify the word in the passage.

Phonemic Awareness *(cont.)*

Sounds: Vowels

Short Vowel Sounds

Short *a*
c<u>a</u>n
h<u>a</u>t

Short *e*
st<u>e</u>p
g<u>e</u>t

Short *i*
w<u>i</u>ll
f<u>i</u>t

Short *o*
st<u>o</u>p
r<u>o</u>ck

Short *u*
b<u>u</u>s
r<u>u</u>n

Long Vowel Sounds

Long *a*
g<u>a</u>ve
m<u>a</u>ke

Long *e*
b<u>e</u>
m<u>e</u>

Long *i*
wh<u>i</u>te
r<u>i</u>de

Long *o*
g<u>o</u>
n<u>o</u>se

Long *u*
h<u>u</u>ge
t<u>u</u>be

Phonemic Awareness (cont.)

Sounds: Consonants

b sound
bus
bike

c sound
can
coat

d sound
did
dark

f sound
fit
roof

g sound
gate
bag

h sound
hello
hike

j sound
jump
jelly

k sound
make
kite

l sound
love
ball

m sound
must
name

n sound
nut
corn

p sound
push
snap

q sound
queen
quiet

r sound
rush
card

s sound
sun
bus

t sound
test
bite

v sound
vest
give

w sound
warm
woke

x sound
next
fox

y sound
yes
yams

z sound
zoo
maze

Phonemic Awareness (cont.)

Sounds: Digraphs

Words to Know

vowel digraph—two vowels in a word that, together, make one sound

ai
long /a/ sound
r<u>ai</u>n
t<u>ai</u>l

ay
long /a/ sound
d<u>ay</u>
w<u>ay</u>

ea
long e
<u>ea</u>t
r<u>ea</u>d

ee
long /e/ sound
b<u>ee</u>
sl<u>ee</u>p

oa
long /o/ sound
b<u>oa</u>t
c<u>oa</u>l

oo
two different sounds
1. l<u>oo</u>k   t<u>oo</u>
2. g<u>oo</u>d   sch<u>oo</u>l

Words to Know

consonant digraph—two consonants in a word that, together, make one sound

ch
mu<u>ch</u>
ca<u>tch</u>

sh
<u>sh</u>oe
fi<u>sh</u>

th
two sounds
1. <u>th</u>ey   <u>th</u>is
2. <u>th</u>ink   wi<u>th</u>

wh
<u>wh</u>en
<u>wh</u>ite

Phonemic Awareness (cont.)

Sounds: Dipthongs and Blends

Word to Know

dipthong—paired vowels or a vowel-consonant pair that makes a single sound

ew	**ou**	**ow**	**oy**
fl<u>ew</u>	h<u>ou</u>se	br<u>ow</u>n	b<u>oy</u>
n<u>ew</u>	<u>ou</u>t	c<u>ow</u>	t<u>oy</u>

Word to Know

blend—two or more consonant sounds together in a word; each consonant keeps its own sound

bl	**br**	**fl**	**fr**
<u>bl</u>ack	<u>br</u>ing	<u>fl</u>ew	<u>fr</u>iend
<u>bl</u>ue	<u>br</u>own	<u>fl</u>y	<u>fr</u>og

gl	**gr**	**nd**	**ng**	**nt**
<u>gl</u>ad	<u>gr</u>ass	a<u>nd</u>	lo<u>ng</u>	a<u>nt</u>
<u>gl</u>ass	<u>gr</u>ow	frie<u>nd</u>	sa<u>ng</u>	we<u>nt</u>

sk	**st**	**tr**	**spr**	**str**
a<u>sk</u>	li<u>st</u>	<u>tr</u>ain	<u>spr</u>ing	<u>str</u>ap
<u>sk</u>ate	<u>st</u>op	<u>tr</u>ick	<u>spr</u>out	<u>str</u>eam

Name: _____

Phonemic Awareness (cont.)

The Lost Book
The Hunt

Kate looked inside her backpack. She could not find her book. She began looking for the book in her room. She looked in her closet and toy box and on her desk. Then she looked all over the house. She looked on top of the table and under the couch. She could not find her library book. It was library day at school. She needed to find the book. "Mom, have you seen my library book?" she asked.

"Where did you have it last?" asked Mom.

"I was reading it in my room."

"I would look there first," said Mom.

Kate went into her room again. She looked in her closet again. Then she looked in her toy box and on her desk. *I give up,* she thought. Kate sat down on the floor. She was worried that she would have to pay for the lost book. She wished very hard that she could find it. "I must find it," she said to herself.

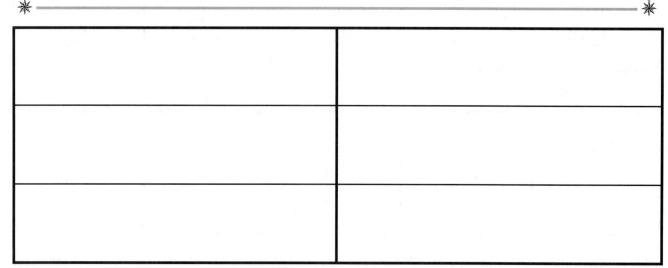

Phonemic Awareness (cont.)

The Lost Book (cont.)

The Plan

Kate finally decided to look under her bed. When she lifted up the bedspread, she saw the book's dark cover. There it was!

"I found it!" she called to her mom. She jumped up and took the book to show her mom. She was glad she had found it.

"We need to take better care of our books next time," explained Mom. "When you bring home a library book, you need to take it out of your backpack. Then put it in the basket on top of your desk," she said.

Kate listened to every word she said. Kate agreed that from now on she would put her library books in the basket on her desk.

She took out a marker and wrote the words "My Library Books" on a sheet of paper to make a sign. Then she taped the sign to the basket. "Now I will remember where to put my library books." She took her library book back to the school library that day.

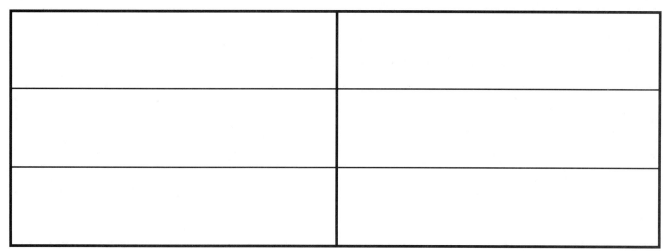

Reading Basics

Skill 3: The student will know that print moves from left-to-right across the page and top-to-bottom.

Instructional Preparation

Materials:

- a big book
- a roll of highlighter tape (*optional*)

Duplicate the following (one per student, unless otherwise indicated):

- "The Lion Family" passage
- "Knowing How to Read" handout

Prepare a transparency of the following:

- "The Lion Family" passage
- "Knowing How to Read" handout

Recall

Before beginning the **Review** component, display a page in a big book for the students to view and facilitate a discussion based on the following questions:

- ✳ Where is the first word you would read on this page? (*in the upper left corner*)
- ✳ Where is the first letter in this word? (*Responses will vary, but should be the first letter of the word.*)
- ✳ How would you read this sentence on this page? (*from left to right*)
- ✳ What would you read next on this page? (*Responses will vary, but should be the second sentence on the page.*)
- ✳ Where is the last word on this page? (*in the bottom right corner*)

Optional: Have students demonstrate finding the letters and words on the page by using a pointer or highlighter tape.

Review

1. Distribute copies of "The Lion Family" passage. Read the passage aloud while the students read it silently.

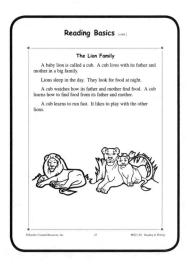

Reading Basics *(cont.)*

Review *(cont.)*

2. Display "The Lion Family" transparency. Ask the following question:

   ✸ What is the first word in the title? (*The*)

   Ask a volunteer to come to the overhead projector and point to the first word in the title. Guide the volunteer to the correct word if necessary. Have him or her take a transparency marker and circle the first word in the title. Tell the other students to do the same on their copy of the passage.

3. Ask the following question:

   ✸ What is the second word in the title? (*Lion*)

   Ask another volunteer to come up and point to the second word in the title. Have the volunteer underline the second word in the title. Tell the other students to do the same on their copy of the passage.

4. Ask the following question:

   ✸ What is the last word in the title? (*Family*)

   Ask a volunteer to come to the overhead projector, point to the last word in the title, and underline the last word in the title. Have the other students do the same on their copy of the passage.

5. Ask another volunteer to come to the overhead projector and point to the words as they read the title to the class. Provide guidance if necessary.

6. Ask the following question:

   ✸ In which direction on the page did [name of volunteer] read the title of the story? (*from left to right*)

   Discuss the students' responses. Guide the class to the understanding that when we read, we always move from left to right along the line of print. Demonstrate by pointing to the title of the passage from left to right on the displayed transparency.

7. Ask the following question:

   ✸ Where is the title of the story found on this page? (*at the top of the page*)

   Ask a volunteer to come and point to the top of the page.

8. Ask the following question:

   ✸ Where is the bottom of the page?

   Ask another volunteer to come and point to the bottom of the page. Model and explain to the students that as we read from left to right across a page, we also move down the page from top to bottom.

Reading Basics (cont.)

Review (cont.)

9. Ask the following question:

   ✻ Where do we read after *and*, the last word in the first line?

   Ask a volunteer to come up and point to the word *mother*. If necessary, guide the student to the correct word. Model and explain that we read from the end of one line of words to the beginning of the next line of words.

10. Distribute copies of the "Knowing How to Read" handout and display the transparency. Read the directions to the students as they follow along silently.

11. Ask a volunteer to read the first question aloud as the other students read along silently. Discuss the students' responses. Display "The Lion Family" transparency again. Find and circle the first word in the sentence with a transparency marker. Tell the students to do the same on their copy of the passage. Display the "Knowing How to Read" transparency again. Record the word *A* on the line in the first box. Have the students do the same on their copy of the handout.

12. Ask a volunteer to read the second question aloud as the other students read along silently. Discuss the students' responses. Display "The Lion Family" transparency again. Find and underline the first sentence. Tell the students to do the same on their copy of the passage. Display the "Knowing How to Read" transparency again. Record the first sentence, "A baby lion is called a cub," on the lines in the second box. Have the students to do the same on their copy of the handout.

13. Put the students in pairs. Tell them to work with their partner to complete their handout. As the pairs complete the handout, have them to read the passage together. Tell them to track the words with their fingers as they read.

14. In a whole-group setting, ask volunteers to read aloud the remaining questions and their answers to the questions. Discuss their answers for accuracy. Record correct answers on the "Knowing How to Read" transparency.

Wrap-Up

- To conclude this lesson, have the students respond orally to the following question: *How do we read the words on a page?*

- Discuss the students' responses for accuracy. Use their responses to review that when we read, we move from left to right across the page and from top to bottom down the page.

Reading Basics (cont.)

The Lion Family

A baby lion is called a cub. A cub lives with its father and mother in a big family.

Lions sleep in the day. They look for food at night.

A cub watches how its father and mother find food. A cub learns how to find food from its father and mother.

A cub learns to run fast. It likes to play with the other lions.

Name: _____

Reading Basics (cont.)

Knowing How to Read

Directions: Read each question below. Write your answer to each question on the lines. Use "The Lion Family" story to help you.

1. What is the first word in the story?

   _____

2. What is the first sentence in the story?

   _____

   _____

   _____

3. What is the last word in the story?

   _____

4. What is the last sentence in the story?

   _____

   _____

   _____

Parts of a Book

Skill 4: The student will recognize that different parts of a book such as the cover, title page, and table of contents offer information.

Instructional Preparation

Materials:

- examples of big books and regular-sized books of fiction and nonfiction, including examples of books with a table of contents

Prepare the following:

- sets of word cards that each contain one of the following words or phrases: title, title page, table of contents (*one set per group of three*)

Duplicate the following (one per student, unless otherwise indicated):

- "Parts of a Book" handout (*one per student*)

Recall

Before beginning the **Review** component, facilitate a discussion based on these questions:

- Why is it important to know the different parts of a book? (*to help a reader get involved with the story; to help a reader predict what a book may be about; to tell a reader information about the book; etc.*)
- Why is it important to know the purpose of the parts of a book? (*to help a reader find particular books; to help a reader find information in the book; to help a reader know the topic of the book; to help a reader find other books by the same author; etc.*)

Review

1. Have the students sit on a rug in the front of the classroom. Display a fictional big book for them to view. Ask a volunteer to come up to the front of the class and point to the front cover of the displayed book. Ask the following questions:

    - What information do you find on the front cover of this book? (*title, author, picture of what the book is about, etc.*)
    - Why is this information important? (*The title tells the reader the name of the book; the title tells the reader what the book is about; the author's name tells the reader who wrote the book; the picture shows the reader what the book will be about and who is in the book.*)

    Discuss the students' responses. Explain that the front cover of the book shows the reader the title of the book, the author of the book, and a picture of what the book will be about. Model pointing to the different parts of the book as you read them aloud. Discuss what those parts are and the importance of that information for the reader.

2. Turn to the title page of the book. Ask a different volunteer to come up and point to the title page of the book, guiding him or her if necessary. Ask the following questions (below and on page 28):

    - What information do you find on the title page of this book? (*The title of the book; the author of the book; another picture that tells more about the book or that may provide the character(s) in the setting of the book.*)

Parts of a Book (cont.)

Review (cont.)

* Why is this information important? (*It is different from the cover of the book; it introduces the setting along with the character(s) in the book.*)
* How is the title page the same as the front cover? (*It tells the title of the book; it tells the author of the book.*)
* How is the title page different from the front cover? (*It shows a different picture of the setting and characters.*)

Discuss the students' responses. Explain that the title page is the first page after the front cover. It shows the title and author of the book and introduces the reader to the setting of the book. Model pointing to the title, author, and picture on the title page as you talk about each feature of the title page.

3. Display a nonfiction big book that includes a table of contents page for the students to view. Briefly discuss the information on the front cover of the book.

4. Turn to the title page of the nonfiction book. Briefly discuss the information on the title page and how it differs from the front cover by including a picture of the book's setting.

5. Turn to the table of contents page of the nonfiction book. Ask a different volunteer to come up and point to the table of contents of the book, guiding the volunteer if necessary. Ask the following questions:

    * What information do you find on the table of contents page of this book? (*list of names of sections in the book and the page number on which the sections begin*)
    * Why is this information important? (*This is a book that includes different sections; the sections of the book and the pages on which they begin are listed; the book is organized into different sections.*)

Discuss the students' responses. Explain that the table of contents page is included to show that the book has many sections. The table of contents shows the title of each section and the page number on which it begins. Model pointing to the title of a section in the table of contents and the page number on which the section begins as you read it aloud to the students. Then model finding that section in the book.

6. Ask other volunteers to look at the table of contents of the displayed book to find other specific sections and the pages on which they begin. Guide the volunteers as necessary.

7. Have the students get into groups of three. Distribute examples of fiction books, nonfiction books, and a set of three word cards. Tell them to place the books and the three word cards facedown in front of them. Model as you explain that each student will take a turn choosing a word card, reading it aloud to the group, choosing a book, and showing to the group the part of the book that is on the word card. Tell the groups to discuss each student's answer. Have each student return the book to the middle, place his or her word card facedown, and mix the cards for the next student to draw.

Wrap-Up

* To conclude this lesson, have the students get into pairs. Distribute the "Parts of a Book" handout. Tell the students to work with their partner to complete the handout.
* In a whole-group setting, ask volunteers to read and explain their responses to the class. Discuss their responses for accuracy. Use their responses to review the parts of a book and the information they provide.

Name: _____

Parts of a Book (cont.)

Reference Sheet

The front cover of a book tells me

_____

_____

The title page of a book tells me

_____

_____

The table of contents of a book tells me

_____

_____

Letter Sounds

Skill 5: The student will demonstrate understanding of the sounds of letters and understanding that words begin and end alike (onsets and rimes).

Instructional Preparation

Choose or prepare the following:

- alphabet cards (*one different letter card per student; create your own cards or duplicate the ones provided on pages 114–139*)

Duplicate the following (one per student, unless otherwise indicated):

- "My Cat" passage
- "Words that Sound the Same" handout

Recall

Before beginning the **Review** component, facilitate a discussion based on the following questions:

* Why is it important to know the sounds of letters in words? (*to help sound out a word; to figure out an unfamiliar word*)

* Why is it important to know the beginning letter sound in words? (*to know the sound a word begins with; to identify other words that begin with the same sound; to match objects with words that begin with the same sound; to find pictures that begin with the same sound; to spell words correctly*)

* Why is it important to know the ending letter sounds in words? (*to know the sounds a word ends with; to recognize rhyming words; to match objects with words that end with the same sounds; to find pictures that end with the same sound as a word; to spell words correctly*)

Review

1. In advance, hide the prepared alphabet cards around the classroom. Have the students sit for circle time. Tell them that they are going to play a game called Letter Hunt. Have each student find one alphabet card hidden in the classroom. Then tell them to return to the circle after they have found a letter card.

2. Have each student identify the sound that matches his or her letter. Then have him or her say a word that begins with that letter. Discuss with the students how important it is to know letter sounds to help them figure out words.

3. Distribute copies of the "My Cat" passage. Read the passage aloud while the students read along silently.

4. Ask the following question:

    * What is a word in the story that begins with the /b/ sound? (*best, ball, box, book, but, be*)

    Discuss the students' responses. Record the correct words on the classroom board or on a sheet of chart paper.

Letter Sounds (cont.)

Review (cont.)

5. Record the word *best* on the classroom board or on a sheet of chart paper, separating the initial consonant letter (onset) from the rest of the word (rime): *b-est*. Ask:

   * What is a word that rhymes with the word *best*? (*Responses will vary; accept all reasonable responses of words that rhyme with "best."*)

   Discuss the responses. Record the appropriate rhyming words beneath the word *b-est* on the classroom board or sheet of chart paper.

6. Ask the following question:
   * How do you know if a word rhymes with another word? (*The letters sound the same at the end of the words; the ending letters in the words are spelled the same.*)

   Discuss the students' responses. Explain that rhyming words sound the same and are spelled the same at the end of the words. Underline the rime in each word listed. Tell them that the beginning sounds are different in each word listed. Circle the beginning letter in each word listed.

7. Have the students listen to the ending sounds in each word as you read the list of rhyming words together.

8. Distribute copies of the "Words that Sound the Same" handout. Tell the students that they will practice writing rhyming words. Read the words in all of the boxes aloud while they read along silently.

9. Explain to the students that they will write two rhyming words for each word listed in a box. Show this on your copy of the handout. Remind them to think about the ending letters in the word as they make rhyming words. Direct their attention to the first box. Ask a volunteer to read the word aloud while the other students read it silently. Ask the following question:
   * What is a word that rhymes with the word *pet*? (*Accept all reasonable responses.*)

   Discuss the responses. Tell the students that the correct responses are words that have the same ending as the word *pet*. Underline the rhyme in each correct response.

10. Model writing a correct response on the line in the first box on the handout. Tell the students to write the same word on the line in the same box on their copy of the handout. Repeat this procedure with another example of a rhyming word for the word *pet*.

11. Have the students get into pairs. Tell them to work with their partner to complete the handout according to the first example.

12. In a whole-group setting, ask volunteers to read the rhyming words for the rest of the words on the handout. Discuss their responses for accuracy. Tell the students to check their handout and make changes as needed. Review the importance of knowing letter sounds and the onset and rime of words.

Wrap-Up

- To conclude this lesson, have the students respond orally to the following questions: *Why is it important to know letter sounds in words? Why is it important to know rhyming words?*

- Ask volunteers to explain their responses to the class and use their responses to review the importance of knowing letter sounds in words and rhyming words.

Letter Sounds (cont.)

My Cat

I have a pet. It is a cat. My cat is all white. I call her Snowy. Snowy is my best friend.

Snowy and I like to play. We like to play with a ball of yarn. I roll it to Snowy. She likes to roll it around. We like to play with a box, too. Snowy likes to climb into the box. Then I try to find her.

We like to read books together. Snowy likes to jump on my lap. I read a book to her. She likes to look at the pictures in the book.

Then Snowy jumps down and she is gone. But where did Snowy go? I look all over for her. Then I find Snowy behind the white chair. She likes to play hide-and-seek.

Snowy and I like to be together. She is my best friend. I am glad I have my cat.

Name: _____

Letter Sounds *(cont.)*

Words that Sound the Same

pet	play	look
_____	_____	_____
_____	_____	_____
cat	box	jump
_____	_____	_____
_____	_____	_____
like	ball	down
_____	_____	_____
_____	_____	_____

Letter and Sound Sequence

Skill 6: The student will demonstrate understanding that the sequence of letters in the written word represents the sequence of sounds in the spoken word.

Instructional Preparation

Materials:

- a magnetic board
- uppercase and lowercase magnetic letters, such as the letters in the chosen individual words from the story
- scissors (*one pair per student*)
- small envelopes (*one per student*)

Choose or prepare the following:

- "Rex's Week" passage on a sheet of chart paper
- "Word Cards" page, with each card cut out (*laminate for durability, if possible*)

Duplicate the following (one per student, unless otherwise indicated):

- "Words I Know" handout

Recall

Before beginning the **Review** component, write a familiar one-syllable word, such as *cat*, on the classroom board. Facilitate a discussion based on the following questions:

* What is the first letter in this word? (*c*)
* What is the second letter in this word? (*a*)
* What is the last letter in this word? (*t*)
* What does this word say? (*cat*)
* How do you know this? (*by saying the sounds of the letters in order in the word; by reading the letters left to right in the word*)

Review

1. Have the students sit on the classroom rug. Display the "Rex's Week" story on the chart stand for the class to view. Read the story aloud while the students read along silently. Be sure to track each word with your finger or pointer. Discuss what they think happened on Saturday.

2. Have ready the set of cards that you have cut out from the "Word Cards" page. Display the "Rex" card on the chart stand or the classroom board tray. Display the magnetic board and the set of magnetic letters in front of the students. Ask the following question:

    * What is the first letter in this word? (*R*)

    Ask a volunteer to find the letter and place it on the magnetic board. Guide him or her to choose the correct letter if needed. Have the student compare his or her letter to the first letter on the word card to confirm the correct letter.

Letter and Sound Sequence *(cont.)*

Review *(cont.)*

3. Ask the following question:
   * What is the second letter in this word? *(e)*

   Ask another volunteer to find the letter and place it on the magnetic board; if needed, guide him or her to choose the correct letter. Have the student compare his or her letter to the second letter on the word card to confirm the correct letter.

4. Ask the following question:
   * What is the last letter in this word? *(x)*

   Have another volunteer find the letter and place it on the magnetic board. Guide the student to choose the correct letter, if needed, and have him or her compare the letter to the last letter on the word card to confirm the correct letter.

5. Say the name of each letter in the word *Rex* as you track it with your finger or pointer. Have the students do the same as you track each letter with your finger or pointer. Ask the following question:
   * How do we read the letters in a word? *(from left to right)*

   Discuss the responses. Guide the class to the understanding that we read the letters in a word from left to right.

6. Read the word *Rex* aloud as you place your hand under it or point to the word using a pointer. Have the students do the same as you use your hand or pointer under the word *Rex*.

7. Continue to have the students identify the correct letters and sounds of the other word cards from the story. Use as many word cards from the story as necessary until the students can demonstrate understanding of the sequence of letters and sounds in words.

Wrap-Up

- To conclude this lesson, distribute copies of the "Words I Know" handout, the scissors, and the envelopes. Read the directions on the handout aloud while the class reads along silently. Tell the students to cut out each letter box with their scissors.

- Put the students in pairs. Tell them to take turns making one of the words from the box with the cutout letters and reading it to their partner. Continue this activity for as long as time allows. Circulate among the pairs to assess students' ability to sequence letters and sounds in words. Have the students put the cutout letters in their envelope along with the word box and put the envelope in their desk. You may want to put an extra set of letters with the word box in an envelope along with a copy of the "Rex's Week" passage in a center for a center time activity.

Letter and Sound Sequence (cont.)

Rex's Week

Rex was having a busy week. He was trying to play with or sniff things in the house. Then something always happened.

On Sunday, Rex played with the newspaper. There was newspaper all over!

On Monday, Rex sniffed a plant, and over it went. There was dirt all over!

On Tuesday, Rex played with my slippers. There were bits of my slippers all over!

On Wednesday, Rex sniffed at the dish of cat food. There was cat food all over!

On Thursday, Rex played with a pail of water. There was water all over!

On Friday, Rex sniffed in the trashcan, and over it went. There was trash all over!

On Saturday, Rex found an old box of junk we had stored in the closet. What do you think happened?

Letter and Sound Sequence (cont.)

Word Cards

Rex	He
On	my
and	at
in	it
cat	can

Name: _____

Letter and Sound Sequence (cont.)

Words I Know

Rex	On	in
and	it	my
He	cat	
can	at	

Directions: Cut out each letter below on the dotted lines. Use the letters to make the words from the box. Make each word on the black line above.

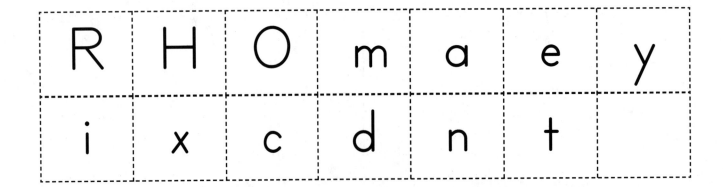

Rhymes and Repeated Sounds

Skill 7: The student will identify the musical elements of literary language such as its rhymes or repeated sounds.

Instructional Preparation

Choose or prepare the following:

- a poem that contains rhyming words and alliteration

Duplicate the following (one per student, unless otherwise indicated):

- "Rhymes and Repeated Sounds" handout
- "Pat's Wig" poem
- "Organizing Words" handout (*one per student pair*)

Prepare a transparency of the following:

- the selected poem
- "Rhymes and Repeated Sounds" handout
- "Pat's Wig" poem
- "Organizing Words" handout

Recall

Before beginning the **Review** component, display the selected poem containing rhyming words and alliteration. Read the poem aloud as the students read along silently. Facilitate a discussion based on the following questions:

- ✻ What do you notice about the sounds of the words used in the poem? (*Some of the words rhyme and some of the words begin with the same sound.*)
- ✻ Which words from the poem rhyme? (*Responses will vary; accept all reasonable responses.*)
- ✻ Which words have the same beginning sound? (*Responses will vary; accept all reasonable responses.*)

Have the students assist you in writing appropriate responses on the classroom board under the proper headings of "Rhyming Words" or "Repeated Beginning Sounds."

Review

1. Distribute copies of the "Rhymes and Repeated Sounds" handout and display the transparency. Read the sentence that begins the first section aloud while the students read along silently. Read aloud the first set of words and point out that the three words rhyme because they have the same ending sound. Ask the following question:

   - ✻ What other words rhyme with *name*, *game*, and *came*? ("*fame*," "*lame*," "*same*," "*tame*," etc.)

©Teacher Created Resources, Inc. 39 #6221 ES: Reading & Writing

Rhymes and Repeated Sounds (cont.)

Review (cont.)

2. Discuss the responses from Step 1 for accuracy, writing appropriate responses on the transparency. Have the students write the responses on their handout. Complete the handout in this same fashion, filling in the lines provided in the rhyming section with rhyming words and the lines provided in the repeated sounds section with words that have the same beginning sound and will complete the phrase.

3. Distribute copies of the "Pat's Wig" poem and display the transparency. Read the poem aloud as the students read along silently. Ask the following questions:

   * What are two of the words from the poem that rhyme? (*An appropriate response is as follows: wig and pig.*)

   * How do you know that they rhyme? (*An appropriate response is as follows: both words end in the same sound.*)

   * What is a phrase that repeats the same beginning sound? (*An appropriate response is as follows: "Proud pink Pat!"*)

   * What is the sound that is repeated in the phrase? (*An appropriate response is as follows: the "p" sound.*)

   Discuss the responses for accuracy. Use the responses to emphasize how to identify words that rhyme and repeated sounds in a passage.

4. Place the students in pairs. Distribute copies of the "Organizing Words" handout and display the transparency. Guide the pairs in completing a section of each organizer using the responses from the previous step that identified a set of rhyming words and a phrase with a repeating beginning sound. Then have the pairs complete each organizer. When the pairs have finished, select volunteers to share responses. Discuss the responses for accuracy and record them on the transparency.

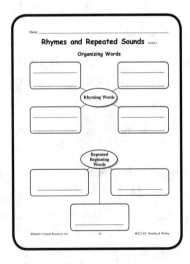

Wrap-Up

* To conclude this lesson, have the students respond orally to the following question: *How can you identify rhyming words and phrases that repeat sounds?*

* Discuss the students' responses for accuracy. Use their responses to review how rhyming words and phases that repeat sounds are identified.

Name: _____

Rhymes and Repeated Sounds *(cont.)*

Rhymes and Repeated Sounds

Rhyming words share the same ending sound.

name game came _____

man can ran _____

wet met get _____

Repeated sounds can be at the beginning of words.

Sara sat still slurping soda.

Mike makes mushy _____

People put _____

Pat's Wig

Pat wore a wig.

It was pink like a pig.

Proud pink Pat!

One day a friend said,

"That's funny hair on your head."

Poor Pat pouted!

Pat colored the wig green,

The shade of a string bean.

Pleased Pat paraded!

Pat loves her wig hair,

and it will stay there.

Happy Pat smiles!

Name: _____

Rhymes and Repeated Sounds (cont.)

Organizing Words

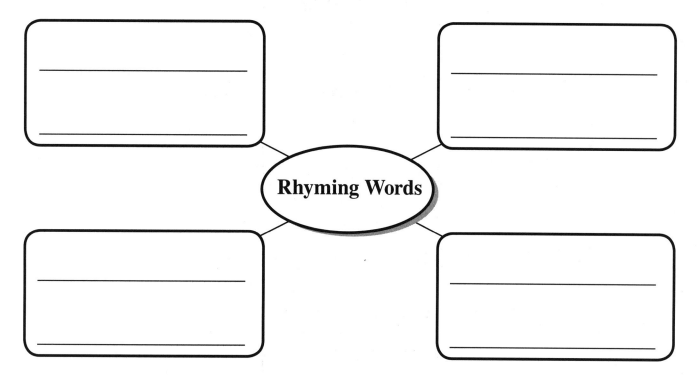

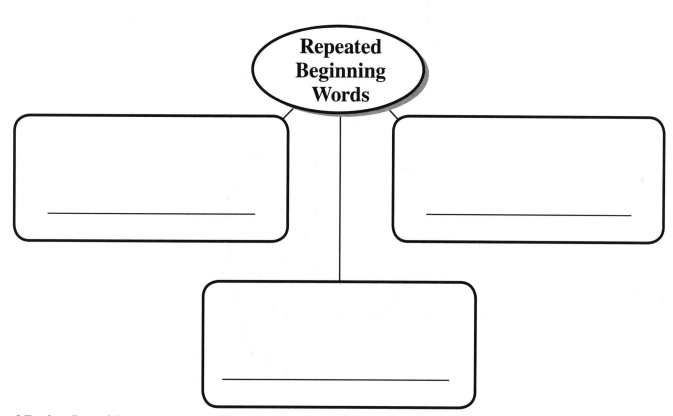

Meaning of Texts

Skill 8: The student will read simple patterned text, decodable text, and/or predictable texts using letter-sound knowledge and pictures to construct meaning.

Instructional Preparation

Choose or prepare the following:

- an unfamiliar, predictable picture book that includes patterned text (e.g., *Alexander and the Terrible, Horrible, No Good, Very Bad Day* by Judith Viorst or *Love You Forever* by Robert Munsch)

Duplicate the following (one per student, unless otherwise indicated):

- "Brown Cow's Party" story
- "Making Meaning" handout

Prepare a transparency of the following:

- "Brown Cow's Party" story
- "Making Meaning" handout

Recall

Before beginning the **Review** component, read aloud half of the chosen picture book and then facilitate a discussion based on the following questions:

* What pictures have been shown in the story? (*Responses will vary.*)
* How can the pictures in the book help the reader? (*Responses will vary but should include that pictures can help the reader identify words used in the text.*)
* What sounds have been used in the story? (*Responses will vary.*)
* How can knowing letters and their sounds help the reader? (*Responses will vary but should include how knowing letters and their sounds can help a reader sound out words.*)
* What pattern of words is repeated in the story? (*Responses will vary.*)
* How can a pattern of words help the reader? (*Responses will vary but should include how patterns can help predict words and content of a story.*)

Discuss the responses for accuracy, emphasizing that a reader uses various strategies to help him or her understand what is being read.

Review

1. Display only part A of the "Brown Cow's Party" transparency, keeping the rest of the story covered. Read the section aloud while the students read it silently. Ask these questions:

    * What pictures are shown in this part? (*a calendar, a birthday cake, a cow, and a telephone*)
    * How do the pictures help the reader? (*The pictures help the reader predict words that will be in the text.*)

    Write appropriate responses on the classroom board. Point out to the students how pictures can help the reader by cueing him or her to expect certain words in the text.

Meaning of Texts *(cont.)*

Review *(cont.)*

2. Point to the letter *c* in the word *call* and ask the following questions:
   * What letter is this? *(the letter "c")*
   * How can knowing the sound that c makes, along with the picture, help the reader figure out how to read this word? *(Knowing that "c" can make the /k/ sound and seeing the picture of the cow on the phone could help a reader figure out that the word is "call.")*

   Write appropriate responses on the classroom board. Emphasize how readers can use letter-sound knowledge and pictures to help them read words.

3. Underline the last two sentences in the section on the transparency. Tell the students that these lines are repeated in the passage. Ask the following question:
   * How can knowing that these sentences are repeated throughout the story help the reader? *(Knowing that the sentences are a repeated pattern throughout the text can help the reader predict the words in the sentences when they are read again.)*

   Write appropriate responses on the classroom board. Emphasize to the students how patterns in text can help a reader predict words or phrases in the text.

4. Display the "Making Meaning" transparency. Read the directions aloud as the students read them silently. Model how to complete the transparency using the information and responses from steps 1–3.

5. Distribute copies of the "Brown Cow's Party" story and the "Making Meaning" handout. Read aloud the entire story as the students read it silently.

6. Put the students in pairs. Guide the pairs in completing one of its handouts with the information in part B of the story. Then assign each pair of students one of the remaining parts (C–E) to use to complete the other handout.

7. When the pairs are finished, ask volunteers to share their responses. Discuss the responses for accuracy.

Wrap-Up

* To conclude this lesson, have the students respond orally to the following question: *What can a reader use in a story to help him or her understand what he or she is reading?*

* Discuss the students' responses for accuracy. Use their responses to review how readers use patterned and predictable text, letter-sound knowledge, and pictures to help in making meaning while reading.

Meaning of Texts (cont.)

Brown Cow's Party

A

It was Brown Cow's birthday. She wanted to have a party. She knew just what to do. She would call up some of her friends and ask them to the zoo.

Old Brown Cow said, "Moo, moo, it's true! I am going to have a party at the city zoo!"

B

The first call was to Monkey. Monkey said that he would be "monkey, monkey happy" to come to the party.

Old Brown Cow said, "Moo, moo, it's true! I am going to have a party at the city zoo!"

C

The second call was to Kitten. Kitten said that she would be "kitty, kitty happy" to come to the party.

Old Brown Cow said, "Moo, moo, it's true! I am going to have a party at the city zoo!"

Meaning of Texts (cont.)

Brown Cow's Party (cont.)

D

The third call was to Rabbit. Rabbit said that she would be "bunny, bunny happy" to come to the party.

Old Brown Cow said, "Moo, moo, it's true! I am going to have a party at the city zoo!"

E

The fourth call was to Pig. Pig said that he would be "piggy, piggy happy" to come to the party.

Old Brown Cow said, "Moo, moo, it's true! I am going to have a party at the city zoo!"

Name: _____

Meaning of Texts (cont.)

Making Meaning

Directions: Read each question below. Write your answer to each question on the lines.

What picture is in your part?
_____
_____

How does the picture help you as you read?
_____
_____
_____

What are some letters and sounds in your part?
_____
_____

How does knowing these letters and sounds help you read?
_____
_____
_____

What pattern of words is repeated in your part?
_____
_____

How it this helpful to you when you read?
_____
_____
_____

Colors, Numbers, and Shapes

Skill 9: The student will demonstrate knowledge of the vocabulary of school such as numbers, shapes, colors, directions, and categories.

Instructional Preparation

Materials:

- several objects in the following colors: red, yellow, blue, orange, green, purple, black, and brown
- several individual numbers 1–10
- several of the following shapes: circle, triangle, square, and rectangle
- brown bags (*one for teacher use; one per group of four*)
- sets of crayons (*one set per student*)

Choose or prepare the following:

- each brown bag with a variety of shapes, numbers, and colored objects

Duplicate the following (one per student, unless otherwise indicated):

- "Drawing Colors, Numbers, and Shapes" handout

Recall

Before beginning the **Review** component, display one of each color, number, and shape in the front of the room. Facilitate a discussion based on the following questions:

- ✸ What is this color? (*Accept all reasonable responses that correctly name the color.*)
- ✸ What is this number: (*Accept all reasonable responses that correctly name the number.*)
- ✸ What is this shape? (*Accept all reasonable responses that correctly name the shape.*)

Review

1. Put the students in groups of four. Distribute to each group a brown bag that contains several shapes, numbers, and colored objects.

Colors, Numbers, and Shapes (cont.)

Review (cont.)

2. Explain that they will take turns in their group choosing an object from the brown bag and identifying it as a shape, color, or number. Model this by choosing an object from your brown bag and saying what the object is. Tell them to take turns until all the objects have been chosen from the bag. Have them keep the chosen objects in front of them. Circulate among the groups to offer assistance as needed.

3. In a whole-group setting, display the objects from your brown bag for the students to view. Ask the following question:

   ✵ How can these objects be grouped? (*by color, number, and shape*)

   Facilitate a discussion that leads the students to determine how the objects are grouped by color, number, and shape. Ask volunteers to come up one at a time to the display of objects and group the objects by color, number, and shape. Discuss the groupings of objects for accuracy.

4. Have the students return to their same group. Tell them to work together to group the objects in their bag by color, number, and shape. Circulate among the groups to offer assistance as needed.

5. Ask volunteers from each group to explain how they grouped their objects. Check the groupings of objects for accuracy. Review how the students followed directions to group the objects by color, number, and shape.

Wrap-Up

- To conclude this lesson, distribute copies of the "Drawing Colors, Numbers, and Shapes" handout and sets of crayons. Read the title and direction aloud while the students read along silently. Have the students complete the handout.

- In a whole-group setting, ask several volunteers to show and explain one of the groups of pictures of colors, numbers, or shapes. Discuss their pictures for accuracy.

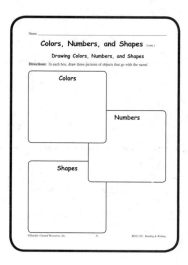

Name: _____

Colors, Numbers, and Shapes *(cont.)*

Drawing Colors, Numbers, and Shapes

Directions: In each box, draw three pictures of objects that go with the name.

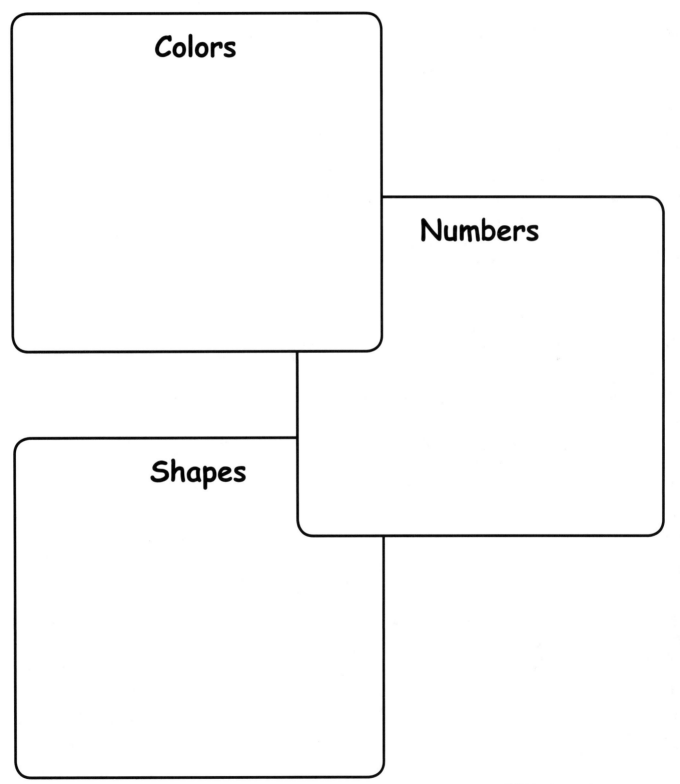

Naming Words and Action Words

Skill 10: The student will identify words that name persons, places, or things, and words that name actions.

Instructional Preparation

Materials:

- a large picture showing a specific person, place, or thing

Duplicate the following (one per student, unless otherwise indicated):

- "Naming Words and Action Words" reference sheet
- "Picnic in the Park" story
- "Identifying Naming and Action Words" handout

Prepare a transparency of the following:

- "Naming Words and Action Words" reference sheet
- "Picnic in the Park" story
- "Identifying Naming and Action Words" handout

Recall

Before beginning the **Review** component, display the picture and have the students study it. Facilitate a discussion based on the following questions:

- ✻ What person is shown in the picture? (*Responses will vary; accept all reasonable responses.*)
- ✻ What place is shown in the picture? (*Responses will vary; accept all reasonable responses.*)
- ✻ What things are shown the picture? (*Responses will vary; accept all reasonable responses.*)
- ✻ What is happening in the picture? (*Responses will vary; accept all reasonable responses.*)

Review

1. Distribute copies of the "Naming Words and Action Words" reference sheet and display the transparency. Read the information aloud while the students read it silently. Write the headings "Naming Words" and "Action Words" on the classroom board. Ask the following questions (below and on page 53):

    - ✻ What are three kinds of naming words? (*words for people, places, and things*)
    - ✻ What are some examples of naming words for people? What are examples of naming words for places? What are examples of naming words for things? (*Responses will vary; accept all reasonable responses.*)

Naming Words and Action Words *(cont.)*

Review *(cont.)*

* What is an action word? *(An action word tells what someone or something is doing.)*
* What are some examples of action words? *(Responses will vary; accept all reasonable responses.)*

Discuss the responses for accuracy. Have the students assist you in using the responses to complete columns of naming and action words under the appropriate headings on the classroom board. Facilitate a discussion with the students that leads to an understanding of how to identify naming words and action words.

2. Put the students in pairs. Distribute copies of the "Picnic in the Park" story and display the transparency. Read the story aloud while the students read it silently. Ask the following questions:

   * What is an example of a naming word from the story? *(Responses will vary; accept all reasonable responses. Examples: school, months, mom.)*
   * What is an example of an action word from the story? *(Responses will vary; accept all reasonable responses. Examples: said, walk, jump.)*

   Discuss the responses for accuracy.

3. Distribute copies of the "Identifying Naming and Action Words" handout and display the transparency. Read the directions aloud as the students read them silently. Use the responses from step 2 to model completing the first two responses on the organizer. Explain to the pairs that they can work together, but that each student needs to complete his or her own copy of the handout.

4. When the pairs are finished, ask volunteers to share their responses. Write appropriate responses on the transparency. Discuss the responses for accuracy.

Wrap-Up

* Conclude the lesson by asking students the following question: *How can you tell if a word is a naming word or an action word?*
* Discuss the students' responses. Use their responses to review how to identify naming words and action words.

Naming Words and Action Words *(cont.)*

Reference Sheet

Naming Words
words that name persons, places, and things

Persons

our names, family names, she, us, I, him

Places

where we live, work, play, and eat

Things

what we can see and touch

Action Words
words that name actions

what people and things do

Naming Words and Action Words *(cont.)*

Picnic in the Park

"There is no school for two months," John said.

His mom asked, "What are you going to do today?"

"I don't know," John said.

"Do you want to have a picnic in the park?" Mom asked.

"That is a great idea," John said. He thought about what he could do at the park. He could play on the slide. He could jump in the sand. Mom made lunch. She put it into a basket.

It was a nice day to walk to the park. John put the basket under a tree. He and his mom ate sandwiches, carrots, and apples. They ate cookies for dessert. John was glad to be out of school.

Name: _____

Naming Words and Action Words *(cont.)*

Identifying Naming and Action Words

Directions: Write words from the story that name a person, place, or thing in the left column under the correct heading. Then write action words from the story in the right column.

	Naming Words	Action Words
Persons		
Places		
Things		

#6221 ES: Reading & Writing

All About "I"

Skill 11: The student will recognize "I" as being the first-person singular pronoun.

Instructional Preparation

Materials:

- lapboards or chalkboards (*one per student pair*)
- pieces of chalk (*one per student pair*)
- socks (for erasing) (*one per student pair*)
- sets of crayons (*one per student*)

Choose or prepare the following:

- a large uppercase cutout of the letter "I" on tagboard (optional), or write the uppercase letter "I" on the classroom board
- the "I" reference sheet written on a sheet of chart paper

Duplicate the following (one per student, unless otherwise indicated):

- "All About Me" passage
- "My Story" handout

Prepare a transparency of the following:

- "All About Me" passage

Recall

Before beginning the **Review** component, facilitate a discussion based on these questions:

✱ What does the word "I" mean? (*It is a word that takes the place of your name.*)

✱ What is a pronoun? (*A pronoun is a word that takes the place of a noun.*)

Display or point to the letter "I" as you ask the first question. Discuss the responses. Explain to the class that the word "I" is a word that takes the place of your name. Say a sentence using your name, and then repeat it using the pronoun "I." Ask volunteers to share an "I" sentence with the class. Write the word *pronoun* on the classroom board. Explain that a pronoun is a word that takes the place of a noun.

Review

1. Display the "I" reference sheet on the chart paper. Read the title and definitions aloud while the students read along silently. Read it again together. Discuss that the pronoun "I" is always a capital, or uppercase, letter.

2. With a colored marker, write a sentence using the pronoun "I" beneath the graphic on the sheet of chart paper. Model writing the pronoun "I" as you write the sentence. Read the sentence aloud while the students read along silently. Ask a volunteer to come up to find and circle the pronoun "I" with another colored marker.

All About "I" (cont.)

Review (cont.)

3. Have the students sit in pairs. Distribute the lapboards, pieces of chalk, and socks. Explain that you will say a sentence using the pronoun "I," and one student in the pair will write the sentence on the lapboard with the piece of chalk. Then the partner will read the sentence aloud and find and circle the pronoun "I" in the sentence. Have the other partner check the sentence for accuracy. Then have the partners exchange roles and repeat the procedure.

4. Continue this procedure with more "I" sentences to allow the students sufficient practice in writing and finding the pronoun "I." Have them put away the lapboards, chalk, and socks.

5. Distribute copies of the "All About Me" passage and a set of crayons. Display the "All About Me" transparency. Explain to the students that they will read a story to practice finding the pronoun "I." Read the passage aloud while the students read along silently.

6. Using the think aloud strategy, model finding the first sentence in the passage that has the pronoun "I" in it. Say the following:

   The first sentence is "My name is James." That does not have the pronoun "I" in it.

   The next sentence is "I am six years old." I see the pronoun "I" in this sentence. I am going to circle it with this red marker.

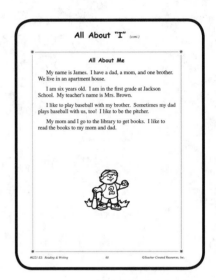

   Tell the students to find the second sentence and circle the pronoun "I" with a red crayon.

7. Have the students continue this procedure of reading each sentence, then finding and circling the pronoun "I" in the rest of the passage.

8. In a whole-group setting, ask volunteers to come up to the displayed passage, find a sentence with the pronoun "I" in it, read it aloud, and use a red transparency marker to circle the pronoun "I." Check for accuracy. Have the students check their story for accuracy.

Wrap-Up

- To conclude this lesson, distribute copies of the "My Story" handout. Read the title aloud while the students read along silently. Explain to them that they will write a story about themselves, using the pronoun "I" in the story. Then have them use the crayons to draw a picture that goes along with their story.

- After the stories are completed, put the students in pairs. Tell them to take turns reading their story to their partner.

- In a whole-group setting, ask several volunteers to read their story and show their picture. Discuss the use of the pronoun "I" in the stories.

All About "I" (cont.)

I is a pronoun.

I is a pronoun that takes the place of your name.

All About "I" *(cont.)*

All About Me

My name is James. I have a dad, a mom, and one brother. We live in an apartment house.

I am six years old. I am in the first grade at Jackson School. My teacher's name is Mrs. Brown.

I like to play baseball with my brother. Sometimes my dad plays baseball with us, too! I like to be the pitcher.

My mom and I go to the library to get books. I like to read the books to my mom and dad.

Name: _____

All About "I" (cont.)

My Story

Comparing Forms of Text

Skill 12: The student will compare different forms of texts such as calendars, newsletters, and signs, and the functions they serve.

Instructional Preparation

Materials:

- a daily classroom schedule, a classroom calendar, and a classroom job list
- 12-by-18-inch sheets of drawing paper (*one per student*)
- sets of colored markers (*one per student*)

Choose or prepare the following:

- classroom signs, similar to the ones on the "Classroom Signs" page, on 9″ x 18″ sheets of construction paper
- a classroom newsletter on a sheet of chart paper

Recall

Before beginning the **Review** component, facilitate a discussion based on these questions:

- What kind of writing or printed material do you see in the classroom? (*lists, signs, names, a calendar, books, maps, etc.*)
- What is the purpose of having the printed material in the classroom? (*to name the jobs in the classroom; to tell who should be doing the jobs; to show the day, month, and year; to show the schedule for the day; to name the different activities and objects in the classroom*)

Review

1. Display a copy of the classroom schedule in front of the students. Ask these questions:
   - What is a classroom schedule? (*the classroom plans for the day, such as reading, writing, spelling, math, gym, music, or computer lab*)
   - What is the purpose of the classroom schedule? (*It shows us the order in which the activities for the day take place.*)

   Facilitate a discussion that leads to the understanding that the classroom schedule is helpful in showing the plans for the day and any special events during the day, such as journaling, library, or silent reading time.

2. Next, display the classroom calendar in front of the students. Ask these questions:
   - What is a classroom calendar? (*a classroom calendar shows the year, month, days of the week, number of days in the month, and classroom happenings, such as birthdays and holidays*)
   - What is the purpose of the classroom calendar? (*It helps us keep track of the days in school; it helps us count the days in a week or month; it shows us special events in a month.*)

   Facilitate a discussion that leads to the understanding that the classroom calendar is helpful in emphasizing events that are meaningful to individual students, and classroom happenings such as birthdays, holidays, or school assemblies. Also, the calendar shows us how many days we have been in school as we count the number of days.

Comparing Forms of Text (cont.)

Review (cont.)

3. Display the classroom job list in front of the students. Ask these questions:

   * What is a classroom job list? (*a list that tells the jobs that need to be done daily in the classroom and the names of the students who are to do a specific job*)

   * What is the purpose of the classroom job list? (*It shows us the jobs that need to be done in our classroom; it shows us who is doing a particular job; etc.*)

   Facilitate a discussion that leads to the understanding that the classroom job list shows the jobs that need to be done in the classroom every day and the name of the classmate who will perform each job. Everyone helps to keep our classroom in order throughout the day.

4. Display the prepared classroom signs on the chalkboard tray in front of the students. Ask the following questions:

   * What are classroom signs? (*signs around the classroom that name objects, such as books, paper, glue, or crayons*)

   * What is the purpose of classroom signs? (*They tell us what the objects are; they help us find particular objects; they help us spell those specific words; they help us read those specific words.*)

   Facilitate a discussion that leads to the understanding that classroom signs name particular objects in the classroom. This helps us to find a particular object in the classroom, because we can look at the picture and read the word on the sign.

5. Display the copy of the classroom newsletter on the sheet of chart paper. Ask the following questions:

   * What is a classroom newsletter? (*The classroom newsletter tells what happened throughout the day or week in the class, such as reading activities, math activities, special people in the class, special events of the class, or science projects.*)

   * What is the purpose of the classroom newsletter? (*It tells the activities that we did for the day or week in our classroom; we share it with our parents so they know what we have done in school; reading the newsletter to our parents gives us practice in reading.*)

   Facilitate a discussion that leads to the understanding that the classroom newsletter tells us what happened in our classroom for the day or week. Explain that when we take it home to share it with our parents, it helps our parents know the different activities we have done at school. It also gives us practice reading the newsletter to our parents.

Wrap-Up

- To conclude this lesson, distribute sheets of drawing paper and sets of colored markers. Have the students illustrate one of the examples of text discussed in the lesson on the sheet of drawing paper using the colored markers. Tell them to write one sentence that tells about the item of text.

- In a whole-group setting, have all the students share their drawing and read their sentence aloud. Discuss the accuracy of the text.

Comparing Forms of Text *(cont.)*

Classroom Signs

books	scissors
puzzles	crayons
glue	paper

Main Idea

Skill 13: The student will read a passage, respond to questions, and discuss the main idea.

Instructional Preparation

Materials:

- highlighters (*one per student*)

Choose or prepare the following:

- a nonfiction book with which the students are familiar

Duplicate the following (one per student, unless otherwise indicated):

- "What a Reader Needs to Know" reference sheet
- "The Blacksmith" passage
- "What's It All About?" handouts

Prepare a transparency of the following:

- "What a Reader Needs to Know" reference sheet
- "The Blacksmith" passage
- "What's It All About?" handouts

Recall

Before beginning the **Review** component, facilitate a discussion based on the following question:

   ✳ What does it mean to find the main idea of a story? (*It means to find out what the story is mostly about.*)

Review

1. To begin this lesson, show the students the cover of the chosen nonfictional book and read its title. Ask the following questions:

   ✳ Who are the [people or animals] in the book? (*Accept all reasonable responses.*)

   ✳ What do the [people or animals] do in the book? (*Accept all reasonable responses.*)

   ✳ When do they do these things? (*Accept all reasonable responses.*)

   ✳ Where are the [people or animals] in the book? (*Accept all reasonable responses.*)

   ✳ Why does [people or animals] [action]? (*Accept all reasonable responses.*)

   ✳ How does [people or animals] [action]? (*Accept all reasonable responses.*)

   ✳ What is the book mainly about? (*Accept all reasonable responses.*)

   Discuss responses for accuracy. Explain to the students that asking and answering these questions help us better understand what we have read. Tell the students that by answering these questions after a book has been read, they can determine whether they have understood the important parts of the book and the main idea of the book.

Main Idea (cont.)

Review (cont.)

2. Distribute copies of the "What a Reader Needs to Know" reference sheet and display the transparency. Read the first box labeled "Who?" Ask for a volunteer to recall the answers given concerning the people or animals in the book. Write details about the people or animals on the classroom board. Continue this procedure by asking volunteers to recall answers for each question. Write the details on the classroom board. Review the details with the children so they remember the *who, what, when, where, why,* and *how* details from the book.

3. Read the box labeled "The Main Idea" on the reference sheet. Ask a volunteer to recall the main idea of the book. Record the main idea on the classroom board. Discuss, using the pictures and title as a means to recall what the book is about. Explain that readers also use the details about the people or animals in the book to help them to know what the book is mainly about.

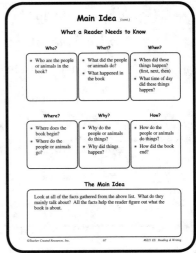

4. Distribute to each student a copy of "The Blacksmith" passage and a highlighter. Display the transparency. Read the passage aloud while the students read along silently. Recall details about the passage to help understand what the passage is about.

5. Distribute to each student a copy of the "What's It All About?" handouts. Read the first question on the handout aloud while the students read it silently. Ask for volunteers to answer the question. Highlight the parts of the passage on the transparency that answer the question. Have the students do the same on their copy of the passage. Tell the students that this is the answer to the first question on the handout. Write the correct answer in the appropriate space on the transparency and have the students do the same on their copy of the handout. Repeat this procedure with the second question.

6. Put the students in pairs. Read aloud the rest of the questions while the students read along silently. Remind the students to find the answer in the passage first and highlight it and then to write their answers on the handout. Have the students complete the remaining questions with their partners. Each student should complete his or her copy of the handout independently, but the pairs should work together to answer the questions.

7. In a whole-group setting, ask volunteers to share their answers. Discuss the responses for accuracy. Write correct responses on the "What's It All About?" transparency.

Wrap-Up

- To conclude instruction, have the students respond aloud to the following questions: *How can you remember and answer questions about what you have just read? What can you do to help you figure out what a book is mainly about?*

- Ask student volunteers to share their responses with the class. Using the students' responses, review the key concepts discussed in the lesson.

Main Idea (cont.)

What a Reader Needs to Know

Who?
* Who are the people or animals in the book?

What?
* What did the people or animals do?
* What happened in the book

When?
* When did these things happen? (first, next, then)
* What time of day did these things happen?

Where?
* Where does the book begin?
* Where do the people or animals go?

Why?
* Why do the people or animals do things?
* Why did things happen?

How?
* How do the people or animals do things?
* How did the book end?

The Main Idea

Look at all of the facts gathered from the above list. What do they mainly talk about? All the facts help the reader figure out what the book is about.

Main Idea (cont.)

The Blacksmith

We use cars to go from place to place. At one time, there were no cars. We rode in wagons pulled by horses. We needed a blacksmith.

A blacksmith makes shoes for horses. He makes wagons, too. He works in a big shop. It holds many tools. It is a hot place.

A blacksmith works with iron. He heats it with fire. This makes it soft. Next, he bends it. Then he shapes it with a hammer. When it is the right size he dips the shoe in water. This cools it down. He nails the shoe to the horse's hoof.

Now we use cars more than horses. There are not as many horses and wagons. A blacksmith is not needed as much as he once was.

Name: _____

Main Idea (cont.)

What's It All About?

Directions: Write the title of the passage. Then read the questions and answer them in the spaces provided.

Title: _____

Who? Who is the story talking about?

_____
_____
_____

What? What does a blacksmith do?

_____
_____
_____

When? When was he needed most?

_____
_____
_____

Name: _____

Main Idea (cont.)

Where? Where did he work?

_____
_____
_____

Why? Why is he not needed now?

_____
_____
_____

How? How does he make horseshoes?

_____
_____
_____

The Main Idea

The story is mainly about . . .

_____
_____

Summarizing Text

Skill 14: The student will demonstrate an ability to summarize text.

Instructional Preparation

Duplicate the following (one per student, unless otherwise indicated):

- "A Butterfly" passage
- "My Summary of a Story" handout

Prepare a transparency of the following:

- "A Butterfly" passage
- "My Summary of a Story" handout

Recall

Before beginning the **Review** component, facilitate a discussion based on the following questions:

* What is a summary? (*the important details and/or ideas*)

* What is a summary of a story? (*The important ideas in the story; the important ideas about the topic of the story; the important ideas in the beginning, middle, and end of the story.*)

* Why is it important to summarize a story? (*to remember what a story is mainly about; to remember the important ideas about the topic of a story*)

Review

1. Distribute copies of the "A Butterfly" passage and display the transparency. Read the title of the passage aloud while the students read along silently.

2. Ask the following question:

    * After reading the title, what do you think this story is about? (*a butterfly*)

    Tell the students to think about the important ideas in the story about the butterfly while they read. Read the passage aloud while they read along silently.

3. Ask a volunteer to read aloud the first paragraph of the passage while the rest of the students read along silently. Ask the following question:

    * What is the most important idea in this paragraph? (*A butterfly is an insect.*)

    Facilitate a discussion that leads to the understanding that the most important idea in this paragraph is that a butterfly is an insect. Underline the first sentence in the passage on the displayed transparency with a transparency marker. Tell the students to underline the same sentence on their copy of the passage.

Summarizing Text *(cont.)*

Review *(cont.)*

4. Ask another volunteer to read aloud the second paragraph of the passage. Ask the following question:

   * What is the most important idea in this paragraph? (*A butterfly has steps in its life.*)

   Facilitate a discussion that leads the students to comprehend that the most important idea in this paragraph is that a butterfly has steps in its life. On the transparency, underline the first sentence in the second paragraph. Tell the students to do the same on their copy of the passage.

5. Ask another volunteer to read aloud the third paragraph of the passage. Ask the following question:

   * What is the most important idea in this paragraph? (*A butterfly has senses.*)

   Discuss that the most important idea in this paragraph is that a butterfly has senses. Underline the first sentence in the third paragraph of the passage. Have the students do the same on their copy of the passage.

6. Ask another volunteer to read aloud the last paragraph of the passage. Ask the following question:

   * What is the most important idea in this paragraph? (*A butterfly likes to fly during the day.*)

7. Distribute copies of the "My Summary of a Story" handout; display the transparency. Read the directions to the students while they read along silently.

8. Ask the following question:

   * What is the first important idea in this story? (*A butterfly is an insect.*)

   Discuss the students' responses. Record the correct response on the writing lines on the displayed transparency. Tell the students to record the same sentence on their copy of the handout.

9. Have the students complete the rest of the summary of the passage, using the information underlined on their passage as a guide.

10. Ask volunteers to read their summary sentences to the class. Discuss their sentences as important ideas of the passage.

Wrap-Up

- To conclude this lesson, read the following passage to the students:

  Every spring, the robin came back. It made its home in the same tree. It sang pretty songs. It let everyone know that winter was over.

- Have the students think about how they would summarize the passage. Ask volunteers to share their summaries with the class. Discuss their responses for accuracy.

Summarizing Text (cont.)

A Butterfly

A butterfly has steps in its life. It begins as an egg. Then the egg hatches into a caterpillar. The caterpillar changes into a butterfly.

A butterfly has senses. It can smell, taste, and touch. It likes to smell, taste, and touch flowers.

A butterfly likes to fly during the day. You will see a butterfly land on flowers and then fly away.

Name: _____

Summarizing Text *(cont.)*

My Summary of a Story

Directions: Write the important ideas from the story on the lines below.

_____

_____

_____

_____

_____

_____

_____

_____

Parts of a Story

Skill 15: The student will demonstrate sense of story (e.g., beginning, middle, end, characters, details, setting).

Instructional Preparation

Materials:

- sheets of butcher paper (*one 3' sheet per student pair*)
- sets of crayons (*one set per student pair*)

Duplicate the following (one per student, unless otherwise indicated):

- "Krista and Marcus" passage
- "A Story Map" handout

Recall

Before beginning the **Review** component, facilitate a discussion based on these questions:

✳ What are the parts of a story? (*characters are the people or animals in a story; setting is where or when a story takes place; the beginning, middle, and end*)

✳ What is a story map? (*an organizer that organizes a story visually; helps recall the parts of the story; helps in sequencing the actions in the story; helps in retelling the story; helps in recalling the details of the story*)

✳ Why is it important to know the parts of a story? (*to help remember what the story is mainly about; to help remember the character(s) in a story; to help remember where and when a story takes place; to help remember the beginning, middle, and end of a story*)

Review

1. Distribute copies of the "Krista and Marcus" passage. Read the passage aloud while the students read along silently. Ask the following question:

   ✳ Who are the characters in this story? (*Krista, Mom, and Marcus*)

   Discuss the names of the characters for accuracy and have the students identify that the characters are people. Circle "Krista," "Mom," and "Marcus" one time each in the story, show the students, and have them circle the names of the characters one time each on their copy of the story.

2. Ask the following question:

   ✳ What is the setting in this story? (*an apartment house*)

   Discuss the responses for accuracy. Remind the students that sometimes authors write only when a story takes place, only where a story takes place, or both when and where a story takes place. Have the students identify that the setting of this story only tells where the story takes place. Tell them to find and circle the words "an apartment house" in the story.

Parts of a Story *(cont.)*

Review *(cont.)*

3. Ask the following question:
   * What happens at the beginning of the story? (*Mom tells Krista that she can find a friend by being herself.*)

   Discuss the responses and what it means to "be yourself." Have the students find and underline the sentence "Mom said, 'Just be yourself.'" in the story.

4. Ask the following question:
   * What happens in the middle of the story? (*Krista goes outside to sit on the steps and begins singing some songs.*)

   Discuss the responses and the reason for Krista's action. Have the students find and underline the following sentences in the story: "Krista went outside to sit on the steps and think. She started singing some songs."

5. Ask the following question:
   * What happens at the end of the story? (*Krista asks Marcus to sing with her, and then they play on a swing.*)

   Discuss the responses for accuracy. Have the students find and underline the following sentences in the story: "Krista asked Marcus to sing with her. Then they both sang and played on the swing together."

6. Distribute copies of the "A Story Map" handout. Read aloud the title and the words in all the boxes while the students read along silently. Tell the students that in the boxes, they will draw pictures that tell about the story.

7. Have the students sit together in pairs. Tell the students to take turns reading the story again, a paragraph at a time, with their partner. Have the students work with their partner to complete their own handout. Remind them to look at the story to help them find the information.

8. In a whole-group setting, ask volunteers to show and explain each part of the story map. Discuss their responses for accuracy. Review with the students that most stories have characters, a setting, a beginning, a middle, and an end.

Wrap-Up

- To conclude this lesson, put the students in pairs. Distribute sheets of butcher paper and sets of crayons. Explain to the students that they are going to use crayons to draw pictures of a story on the sheet of butcher paper. Tell them their story will include characters, a setting, a beginning, a middle, and an end. Have the pairs brainstorm ideas for a story, decide on one idea to use for their short story, and then draw pictures of the characters and setting and the beginning, middle, and end of the story. In a whole-group setting, have all the pairs present and tell about their story. Discuss the stories for characters, setting, a beginning, a middle, and an end. Display the stories on a classroom wall or in the hallway.

Parts of a Story (cont.)

Krista and Marcus

There was a little girl who just moved into an apartment house with her mom. Her name was Krista. Krista was sad because she didn't have anyone to play with her.

One day Krista asked her mom how she could find a friend. Mom said, "Just be yourself."

"All of the other children are afraid of me," said Krista. "I can't even get near them to talk to them."

Krista went outside to sit on the steps and think. She started singing some songs. A little boy lived in the same apartment house. His name was Marcus. He looked out of the window when he heard Krista singing.

Marcus liked Krista's singing. Marcus walked outside. He slowly walked up to Krista to talk to her. Marcus told Krista how much he liked her singing. Krista asked Marcus to sing with her. Then they both sang and played on the swing together. They were both happy that they had found a friend.

Name: _____

Parts of a Story (cont.)

A Story Map

Story Title: _____

Characters (Who?)	Setting (When? Where?)

Beginning of Story

Middle of Story

End of Story

Illustrations

Skill 16: The student will describe how illustrations contribute to a text.

Instructional Preparation

Materials:

- a large poster depicting a scene that involves at least one character

Duplicate the following (one per student, unless otherwise indicated):

- "A New Home" passage
- "Picture Clues" handout

Recall

Before beginning the **Review** component, facilitate a discussion based on these questions:

* What do the pictures in a story tell the reader? (*who the characters are; where and when the story takes place; the events or actions in the story; the topic of a story; what a story will be about*)

* Why is it important to have pictures in a story? (*They help the reader to understand what is happening in the story; they help the reader with the details of the story by telling who, what, where, when, why, and how; the picture details will help the reader remember the sequence of the events in the story.*)

Review

1. Have the students sit on the rug in the front of the classroom. Display the chosen poster on the classroom board. Ask the following question:

   * What does this picture show? (*Responses will vary; accept all responses that reasonably describe the picture.*)

   Discuss the responses. Have the class decide on a reasonable description of the picture. Lead a discussion that helps the students understand that the details in the picture tell who, what, when, where, why, and how. Record the italicized words on the classroom board for the students to reference throughout the lesson.

2. Distribute copies of the "A New Home" passage. Ask the following question:

   * What does the first picture in this story show? (*two birds; two birds looking at each other*)

   Discuss the responses and record them on the classroom board. Tell the students that this picture likely shows who the characters in the story are.

Illustrations (cont.)

Review (cont.)

3. Ask the following question:

    ✳ What does the next picture in this story show? (*a big tree*)

    Discuss the responses; write them on the classroom board. Tell the class that this picture likely shows the what, where, why, or how in the story.

4. Ask the following question:

    ✳ What does the last picture in this story show? (*a bird's nest*)

    Discuss and record the responses as above. Tell the students that this picture likely shows the what, where, why, or how in the story.

5. Explain to the students that they will read a story to practice using the pictures as clues to help them understand and keep track of the details in the story. Read the "A New Home" passage aloud while they read along silently.

6. Put the students in pairs. Distribute copies of the "Picture Clues" handout. Read the title and each question aloud while the class reads along silently. Tell the students to work with their partner to complete their own handout.

7. In a whole-group setting, ask several volunteers to read their descriptions of the pictures from the story. Discuss their descriptions for accuracy. Record appropriate responses for each picture on a sheet of chart paper. Compare and contrast the initial responses on the classroom board to the current responses on the chart paper. Review with the students how picture clues help them to better understand and remember the events in a story.

Wrap-Up

- To conclude this lesson, have the students respond in their writing journals or on the reverse side of their "Picture Clues" handout to the following question: *How do picture clues help a reader to better understand a story?*

- Ask volunteers to read their responses to the class. Discuss their responses for accuracy.

Illustrations (cont.)

A New Home

"We need to make a nest," said Mother Bird. "Soon it will be time for me to lay my eggs."

"Yes," said Father Bird. "I will look for a good place to make a nest." He flew away to look for a good place. Soon he flew back to Mother Bird.

"We can make a nest in this big tree," said Father Bird.

"First, we will need some twigs to make a nest," said Mother Bird. Mother Bird and Father Bird flew to the woods. Father Bird looked under some large trees in the woods. He found some twigs. He took the twigs back to the big tree. Mother Bird looked under some small trees in the woods. She found some twigs. She took the twigs back to the big tree. Mother Bird and Father Bird made a nest with the twigs.

"Now we need something soft for the nest," said Mother Bird.

So, Mother Bird and Father Bird flew to a farm. They found some soft feathers by the duck pond. They took the feathers back to the new nest in the big tree. Mother Bird and Father Bird twisted the feathers into the twigs of the new nest.

"The new nest is ready," said Mother Bird. "Now I can lay my eggs."

Name: _____

Illustrations (cont.)

Picture Clues

What does this picture show?

_____
_____
_____

What does this picture show?

_____
_____
_____

What does this picture show?

_____
_____
_____

Oral-Graphic Directions

Skill 17: The student will follow oral-graphic directions.

Instructional Preparation

Materials:

- scissors (*one per student*)
- 8½ × 11 inch sheets of blank paper (*one per student*)
- glue sticks (*one per student*)
- crayons (one box of eight colors per student)

Duplicate the following (one per student, unless otherwise indicated):

- "Special Shapes" handout
- "Coloring Shapes" handout

Prepare a transparency of the following:

- "Super Dough Recipe" sheet
- "Shape Directions" sheet
- "Coloring Shapes" handout

Recall

Before beginning the **Review** component, facilitate a discussion based on the following question:

> ✴ Why is it important to follow directions? (*Responses will vary; accept all reasonable responses.*)

Discuss the responses to show the importance of following directions.

Review

1. Display the "Super Dough Recipe" transparency. Point out that the recipe gives the directions to make super dough. Read the recipe aloud as the students read it silently. Then ask the following questions (below and on page 84):

    > ✴ Why are the directions for each step in the recipe numbered? (*An appropriate response is as follows: because the steps need to be completed in a particular order.*)

    > ✴ Why do the steps need to be done in a particular order? (*because the super dough will not come out the way it is supposed to if the steps are done in a different order*)

©Teacher Created Resources, Inc.

Oral-Graphic Directions (cont.)

Review (cont.)

* How do the pictures in the recipe help us? (*The pictures help show how much of each ingredient is needed and what needs to be done in the steps.*)
* What could happen if we don't follow all the directions? (*Responses will vary; accept all reasonable responses.*)

Discuss the responses for accuracy. Emphasize the importance of following directions in order and not skipping any parts of the directions. Point out that pictures can give clues to understanding directions.

2. Put the students in pairs. Distribute copies of the "Special Shapes" handout. Give each student a pair of scissors. Explain to the students that they will be using the shapes to make a surprise picture. Tell them that you will be reading the directions aloud to them. Emphasize that they must listen carefully and follow each step of the directions in order without skipping any parts. Explain to the pairs that they will be working together to figure out the directions, but that each student will need to complete his or her own picture.

3. Display the "Shape Directions" transparency. Read aloud the first step in the directions. Give the students time to finish this first step. Then read aloud step 2. Model where to put the rectangles. Continue in this same style for step 3. Then read aloud the remaining steps without modeling. Allow for adequate transition time between each direction.

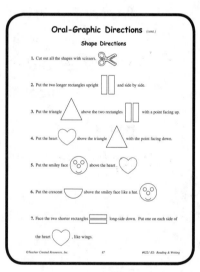

4. Ask several volunteers to share their pictures. Discuss their pictures for accuracy. Display the "Coloring Shapes" transparency. Have the students compare their pictures with the one on the transparency. Review with the students the importance of following directions. Distribute blank sheets of paper and glue sticks and have the students paste the shapes onto the paper in the same order given in the directions.

Wrap-Up

- To conclude this lesson, distribute the "Coloring Shapes" handout and crayons. Give oral directions from the top to the bottom of the page, telling the students what color each shape should be. Then ask the following questions: *What are the directions you need to follow? Why is following directions important?*

- Discuss the responses for accuracy. Use the responses to review the importance of how to follow directions.

Oral-Graphic Directions *(cont.)*

Super Dough Recipe

Ingredients:

- 4 cups flour

- 1 cup salt

- ½ cup grape juice

- 2 cups water

Directions:

1. Pour flour into a big bowl.

2. Add salt and mix.

3. Add grape juice and mix.

4. Slowly stir in water a little at a time until mixture is soft but not sticky.

5. Store mixture in a tight container.

Oral-Graphic Directions (cont.)

Special Shapes

Oral-Graphic Directions (cont.)

Shape Directions

1. Cut out all the shapes with scissors.

2. Put the two longer rectangles upright and side by side.

3. Put the triangle 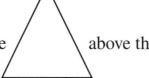 above the two rectangles with a point facing up.

4. Put the heart above the triangle with the point facing down.

5. Put the smiley face above the heart.

6. Put the crescent above the smiley face like a hat.

7. Face the two shorter rectangles long-side down. Put one on each side of the heart , like wings.

Name: _____

Oral-Graphic Directions *(cont.)*

Coloring Shapes

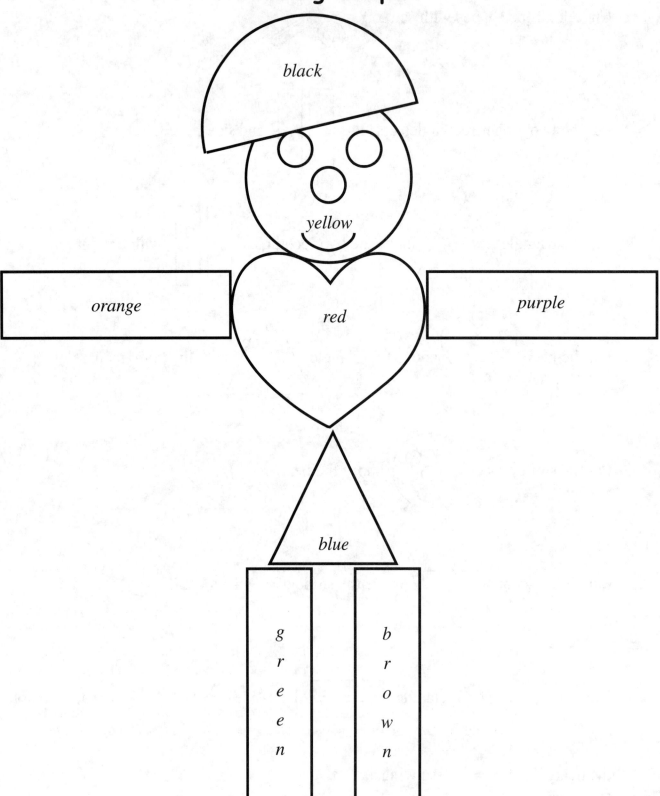

#6221 ES: Reading & Writing

Making Predictions

Skill 18: The student will make predictions about possible events in texts before, during, and after reading.

Instructional Preparation

Materials:
- an unfamiliar picture book

Duplicate the following (one per student, unless otherwise indicated):
- "Making Predictions" reference sheet
- "My Predictions" handout
- "Under the Big Top" story

Prepare a transparency of the following:
- "Making Predictions" reference sheet
- "Under the Big Top" story
- "My Predictions" handout

Recall

Before beginning the **Review** component, show the students the title, cover, and pictures of the picture book. Then facilitate a discussion based on the following questions:

- What do you think will happen in this story? (*Answers will vary; accept all reasonable responses.*)
- What is it called when we guess what the story will be about? (*predicting*)

Discuss the responses to show that it is sometimes possible to make guesses about what will happen in a story by looking at the title, the cover, and the pictures of a picture book.

Review

1. Distribute copies of the "Making Predictions" reference sheet and display the transparency. Read the information on the reference sheet aloud as the students read along silently. Then ask the following questions:

    - How does a reader make predictions before reading a story? (*by looking at the title, the cover, and pictures; thinking about experiences; and making a smart guess*)
    - How does a reader make predictions during the reading of the story? (*by looking at the pictures and the text, thinking about what is happening in the story, and making a smart guess*)
    - How does a reader make predictions after reading a story? (*by looking back at the pictures and the text, thinking about what has happened and what could happen next time, and making a smart guess*)

Making Predictions (cont.)

Review (cont.)

2. Put the students in pairs. Display the "Under the Big Top" transparency and cover the text. Read the title of the story aloud while the students listen and look at the picture in the story. Ask the following question:

   ✳ After seeing the picture in the story and hearing the title, what do you think this story is about? (*Responses will vary; accept all reasonable responses.*)

   Discuss the responses. Explain to the students that they predicted what might happen in the story.

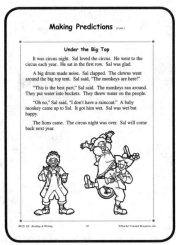

3. Distribute copies of the "My Predictions" handout and display the transparency. Read the first question aloud as the students follow along silently. Ask volunteers to share their predictions. Write an appropriate response on the transparency. Have the students record their predictions in the first section of the handout.

4. Display the first two paragraphs of the "Under the Big Top" story and read them aloud as the students read along silently. Have the students answer the second question on the "My Predictions" handout.

5. Ask volunteers to read their predictions to the class. Discuss their predictions.

6. Distribute copies of the "Under the Big Top" story to the students. Finish reading the story to the students as they read along silently.

7. Have the students complete the last section of the handout on their own.

8. Ask volunteers to read their predictions to the class. Discuss their predictions.

Wrap-Up

- To conclude this lesson, ask the following questions: *How does a reader make predictions when reading a story? How does making predictions help the reader understand the story?*

- Discuss the responses for accuracy. Review how a reader makes predictions before, during, and after reading a passage.

Making Predictions (cont.)

Reference Sheet

Making Predictions Before Reading

Read the title.

Look at the pictures on the cover and inside.

Think about your own experiences.

Make a smart guess.

Making Predictions While Reading

Look at the pictures and text.

Think about what is happening in the story.

Think about what could happen next.

Make a smart guess.

Making Predictions After Reading

Look back at the pictures and text.

Think about what has happened in the story.

Think about what could happen next time.

Make a smart guess.

Making Predictions *(cont.)*

Under the Big Top

It was circus night. Sal loved the circus. He went to the circus each year. He sat in the first row. Sal was glad.

A big drum made noise. Sal clapped. The clowns went around the big top tent. Sal said, "The monkeys are here!"

"This is the best part," Sal said. The monkeys ran around. They put water into buckets. They threw water on the people.

"Oh no," Sal said, "I don't have a raincoat." A baby monkey came up to Sal. It got him wet. Sal was wet but happy.

The lions came. The circus night was over. Sal will come back next year.

Name: _____

Making Predictions *(cont.)*

My Predictions

What do I predict will happen in the story?

What do I predict will happen next?

What do I predict will happen next time?

Asking Questions

Skill 19: The student will ask questions in order to check that he or she understands what was read in a passage.

Instructional Preparation

Choose or prepare the following:

- highlighters (*one per student pair*)

Duplicate the following (one per student, unless otherwise indicated):

- "The Facts of Matter" passage
- "Asking Myself Questions: Part I" handout
- "Asking Myself Questions: Part II" handouts
- "Whooo-ooo Is It?" passage (*one per student pair*)
- "Three Questions" handout

Prepare a transparency of the following:

- "The Facts of Matter" passage
- "Asking Myself Questions: Part I" handout
- "Asking Myself Questions: Part II" handouts

Recall

Before beginning the **Review** component, facilitate a discussion based on these questions:

✱ Why do people ask questions? (*to obtain information*)

✱ How could asking questions help you to understand something you have read? (*Answers will vary. Accept reasonable responses.*)

Review

1. To begin this lesson, tell the students that they will practice reading to find ways to help themselves understand what they have read. Distribute to each student a copy of "The Facts of Matter" passage. Display the "The Facts of Matter" transparency on the overhead projector. Read the passage aloud while the students read it silently.

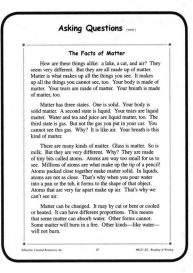

Asking Questions (cont.)

Review (cont.)

2. After reading the passage aloud, ask the students the following questions:
   * What is "The Facts of Matter" passage about? (*matter*)
   * What is the most important idea in the passage? (*Matter is what makes up all the things we see.*)
   * What are some other important details about matter? (*Responses may vary; accept all reasonable responses.*)

3. Field the students' responses to the questions asked in step 2. Circle the answer to the first question and underline the answers to the other two questions on the transparency of the passage. Underline the answer to the second question with a red overhead marker and the answers to the third question with a blue overhead marker. Facilitate a discussion to review how to find the main idea and supporting details in a nonfiction passage.

4. Continue by asking the students the following question:
   * If you wanted to better remember what you just read, what could you do? (*Responses may vary; accept all reasonable responses.*)

   Field the students' responses. Lead the students to the understanding that a reader can ask himself or herself questions to help remember what the passage is about.

5. Distribute to each student a copy of the "Asking Myself Questions: Part I" handout and display the transparency on the overhead projector. Read the directions on the first page aloud to the students while they read them silently. Discuss the directions to make sure the students understand them. Read each of the three questions in the boxes. Ask the students the following questions:
   * Which one of these questions would help you better understand what this story is about? Why?

   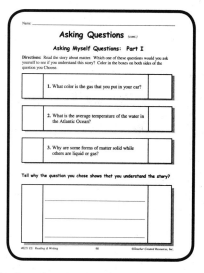

   Field the students' responses. Lead the students to the understanding that the third question would best help them understand the passage because that is the main idea of the passage

6. Model how to complete the first page of the handout by coloring the appropriate boxes and writing in why that question is correct on the transparency of the handout. Have the students color in the boxes on either side of the third question and write why they chose this question in the box at the bottom of their copy of the "Asking Myself Questions: Part I" handout.

©Teacher Created Resources, Inc. 95 #6221 ES: Reading & Writing

Asking Questions (cont.)

Review (cont.)

7. Distribute copies of the "Asking Myself Questions: Part II" handouts and display the transparencies. Ask the students the following question:

   ✷ What other questions would you ask yourself to make sure you understood the information about matter?

   Field the students' responses and discuss them. Then have the student complete both pages of the handout as you circulate around the room and offer assistance. Have students volunteer their questions and discuss them with the class.

8. Have the students assemble in pairs. Distribute to each pair a highlighter and a copy of the "Whooo-ooo Is It?" passage. To each students also distribute a copy of the "Three Questions" handouts.

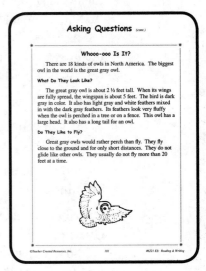

9. Read the passage aloud while the students read it silently. Instruct the pairs to reread the passage, circle what the story is about, underline the main idea, and highlight the supporting details in the passage. Allow adequate time for task completion.

10. Review the directions on the first page of the "Three Questions" handout. Have each group decide on three questions it feels would help the group members better remember the passage. Instruct each member of the group to write these questions in the appropriate boxes on his or her copy of the handouts. Then, tell the groups to write an explanation that tells why each question they wrote shows they understood the passage. Each member of the group should complete his or her own copy of the handouts, but the group members should work together to brainstorm ideas. Allow adequate time for task completion.

11. In a whole-group setting, ask student volunteers to share their questions and explanations aloud with the whole class. Discuss each question and explanation for accuracy. Write selected correct responses on the displayed transparency.

Wrap-Up

- To conclude instruction, have the students respond aloud to the following question: *How does asking yourself questions help you understand what you have just read in a story?*

- Ask student volunteers to share their responses with the class. Using the students' responses, review the key concepts discussed in the lesson.

Asking Questions (cont.)

The Facts of Matter

How are these things alike: a lake, a cat, and air? They seem very different. But they are all made up of matter. Matter is what makes up all the things you see. It makes up all the things you cannot see, too. Your body is made of matter. Your tears are made of matter. Your breath is made of matter, too.

Matter has three states. One is solid. Your body is solid matter. A second state is liquid. Your tears are liquid matter. Water and tea and juice are liquid matter, too. The third state is gas. But not the gas you put in your car. You cannot see this gas. Why? It is like air. Your breath is this kind of matter.

There are many kinds of matter. Glass is matter. So is milk. But they are very different. Why? They are made of tiny bits called atoms. Atoms are way too small for us to see. Millions of atoms are what make up the tip of a pencil! Atoms packed close together make matter solid. In liquids, atoms are not as close. That's why when you pour water into a pan or the tub, it forms to the shape of that object. Atoms that are very far apart make up air. That's why we can't see air.

Matter can be changed. It may by cut or bent or cooled or heated. It can have different proportions. This means that some matter can absorb water. Other forms cannot. Some matter will burn in a fire. Other kinds—like water—will not burn.

Name: _____

Asking Questions (cont.)

Asking Myself Questions: Part I

Directions: Read the story about matter. Which one of these questions would you ask yourself to see if you understand this story? Color in the boxes on both sides of the question you Choose.

	1. What color is the gas that you put in your car?

	2. What is the average temperature of the water in the Atlantic Ocean?

	3. Why are some forms of matter solid while others are liquid or gas?

Tell why the question you chose shows that you understand the story?

_____
_____
_____

Name: _____

Asking Questions (cont.)

Asking Myself Questions: Part II

Directions: Write two more questions you would ask yourself to help remember the information about matter. Then, tell why the question you wrote shows you understood information from the story.

Question #1

Tell why this question shows that you understand the story?

Name: _____

Asking Questions (cont.)

Asking Myself Questions: Part II (cont.)

Question #2

_____

Tell why this question shows that you understand the story?

Asking Questions (cont.)

Whooo-ooo Is It?

There are 18 kinds of owls in North America. The biggest owl in the world is the great gray owl.

What Do They Look Like?

The great gray owl is about 2 ½ feet tall. When its wings are fully spread, the wingspan is about 5 feet. The bird is dark gray in color. It also has light gray and white feathers mixed in with the dark gray feathers. Its feathers look very fluffy when the owl is perched in a tree or on a fence. This owl has a large head. It also has a long tail for an owl.

Do They Like to Fly?

Great gray owls would rather perch than fly. They fly close to the ground and for only short distances. They do not glide like other owls. They usually do not fly more than 20 feet at a time.

Asking Questions (cont.)

Whooo-ooo Is It? (cont.)

How and What Do They Hunt?

The great gray owl hunts mainly in the early morning and late afternoon. But it will also hunt at night. The great gray owl will "sit and wait" when hunting. It hunts using its eyesight. It can also hunt using its hearing alone. It waits. Then it plunges onto its prey.

These owls eat small rodents like voles. They will also eat gophers, rats, mice, squirrels, rabbits, chipmunks, moles, and weasels.

Where Do They Live?

The forests are home to the great gray owls. They may also live on the edges of swamps and forests. They can be found in Alaska, Canada, Minnesota, and the Rocky Mountains. They are also found in Europe and Asia.

Name: _____

Asking Questions *(cont.)*

Three Questions

Directions: Write three questions you would ask yourself to help remember the information about the great gray owl. Then, tell why the question you wrote shows you understood information from the story.

Question #1

Tell why this question shows that you understand the story?

Name: _____

Asking Questions *(cont.)*

Three Questions *(cont.)*

Question #2

[   ]

Tell why this question shows that you understand the story?

[   ]

Name: _____

Asking Questions (cont.)

Three Questions (cont.)

Question #3

Tell why this question shows that you understand the story?

Fiction vs. Nonfiction

Skill 20: The student will state the difference between fiction and nonfiction, including fact and fantasy.

Instructional Preparation

Choose or prepare the following:

- two unfamiliar books (one nonfiction, the other fiction)

Duplicate the following (one per student, unless otherwise indicated):

- "Differences Between Nonfiction and Fiction" reference sheet
- "Boats" passage
- "Nonfiction and Fiction" handout
- "Carrie Meets Frank" story

Prepare a transparency of the following:

- "Differences Between Nonfiction and Fiction" reference sheet
- "Boats" passage
- "Nonfiction and Fiction" handout
- "Carrie Meets Frank" story

Recall

Before beginning the **Review** component, display the chosen books for the students to examine. Read each title aloud and read enough text from each book so that the students can determine the genres. Then facilitate a discussion based on the following question:

- ✹ How can you tell whether the books are nonfiction or fiction? (*Responses will vary but should focus on the following: nonfiction books are true, and fiction books are made up.*)

Review

1. Distribute copies of the "Differences Between Nonfiction and Fiction" reference sheet and display the transparency. Read the information aloud as the students read it silently. Then ask the following questions:

   - ✹ What does *nonfiction* mean? (*something that is real or true*)
   - ✹ What does *fiction* mean? (*something that is made up*)
   - ✹ How can you tell the difference between nonfiction and fiction? (*Responses will vary; accept all reasonable responses.*)

   Discuss the responses for accuracy, focusing on the differences between nonfiction and fiction.

Fiction vs. Nonfiction *(cont.)*

Review *(cont.)*

2. Distribute copies of the "Boats" passage and display the transparency. Read the passage aloud as the students read it silently. Then ask the following questions:

   ✸ Is this passage nonfiction or fiction? (*nonfiction*)

   ✸ What makes the passage nonfiction? (*It is a passage written to give the reader true facts about boats.*)

   ✸ Why is the passage not fiction? (*because the passage is not made up*)

   Discuss the responses for accuracy.

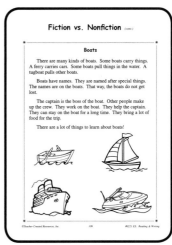

3. Distribute copies of the "Nonfiction and Fiction" handout and display the transparency. Use the responses from step 2 to guide the students in completing the first organizer on the handout.

4. Put the students in pairs. Distribute copies of "Carrie Meets Frank" and display the transparency. Read the story aloud as the students follow along silently. Have the pairs work together to use the information from the story to complete the second organizer on the "Nonfiction and Fiction" handout.

5. When the pairs have finished, redisplay the "Nonfiction and Fiction" transparency. Ask for volunteers to share their responses. Discuss the responses for accuracy and record them on the transparency. Allow students to make corrections to their organizer as needed.

Wrap-Up

- To conclude this lesson, have the students respond on the back of their handout to the following question: *What is the difference between nonfiction and fiction?*

- Discuss their responses for accuracy. Review the importance of knowing the difference and how it helps them understand more about the stories they read.

Fiction vs. Nonfiction (cont.)

Differences Between Nonfiction and Fiction

Nonfiction

passages written to tell facts or a true story

Fiction

passages that describe made-up people and events

- ✵ will have facts
- ✵ will be real life
- ✵ will be true

- ✵ may be a fantasy
- ✵ always made up
- ✵ may seem true

Fiction vs. Nonfiction (cont.)

Boats

There are many kinds of boats. Some boats carry things. A ferry carries cars. Some boats pull things in the water. A tugboat pulls other boats.

Boats have names. They are named after special things. The names are on the boats. That way, the boats do not get lost.

The captain is the boss of the boat. Other people make up the crew. They work on the boat. They help the captain. They can stay on the boat for a long time. They bring a lot of food for the trip.

There are a lot of things to learn about boats!

Name: _____

Fiction vs. Nonfiction (cont.)

Nonfiction and Fiction

Passage Title: _____

This passage is

nonfiction   **fiction**
(circle one)
because

This passage is

nonfiction   **fiction**
(circle one)
because

Passage Title: _____

This passage is

nonfiction   **fiction**
(circle one)
because

This passage is

nonfiction   **fiction**
(circle one)
because

Fiction vs. Nonfiction (cont.)

Carrie Meets Frank

It is morning. Carrie, the cute red car, is happy. Today she will meet Frank. Frank is a ferry boat. He takes cars across the water.

Carrie races around the city. She wants to be the first car to get on the ferry. And she is. She pays the toll, and the crew shows her where to park. She has lunch while she waits for Frank.

The port is big. It takes her breath away. Carrie is scared. Then, she hears a loud, deep voice.

"The port did the same to me the first time I saw it," Frank says.

"How do you know where you are going?" asks Carrie.

"My captain knows the way," Frank says.

Then he laughs and says, "If he forgets, I show him the way home." Carrie laughs too. Carrie is glad she stayed at the port.

Uppercase and Lowercase Letters

Skill 21: The student will name, identify, and write each letter of the alphabet, both upper- and lowercase.

Instructional Preparation

Materials:

- sets of crayons (*one set per student*)
- a chart stand

Prepare the following:

- the upper- and lowercase alphabet cards (pages 114–139); copy each card onto colored cardstock

Duplicate the following (one per student, unless otherwise indicated):

- "Letters of the Alphabet" handouts

Recall

Before beginning the **Review** component, facilitate a discussion based on the following questions:

* What is a letter of the alphabet? (*It is a name for a symbol; it is made with lines, curves, circles, and tails; it has two forms, uppercase and lowercase; each letter makes a sound; some letters make more than one sound in connection with other letters.*)

* Why is it important to learn the letters of the alphabet? (*Letters are used to make words; to be able to read words correctly; to be able to write words correctly.*)

Review

1. Have the cards of uppercase and lowercase letters of the alphabet displayed on a classroom wall so they are accessible to the students. (Use the alphabet cards on pages 114–139. Copy each card onto colored cardstock to add color and durability to the cards.) Have the students sit on the rug in front of the classroom. Tell them to name the letters of the alphabet as you use a pointer and point to each letter in order.

 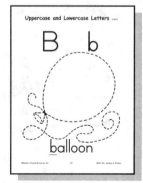 

Uppercase and Lowercase Letters *(cont.)*

Review *(cont.)*

2. Explain to the students that they will play a game called "Name the Letter." Tell them you will point to different letters of the alphabet and they will name the letter. Using the pointer, randomly point to the uppercase and lowercase letters of the alphabet and ask:

   * What is the name of this letter?
   * Is it an uppercase or lowercase letter?

   Discuss the students' responses for accuracy. Continue this activity until everyone has had an opportunity to "Name the Letter."

3. Explain to the students that they will identify letters of the alphabet by their forms, such as lines, curves, circles, and tails. Review each feature by showing an example of each letter. Demonstrate the specific feature of the particular letter by tracing over it with your finger. Tell the students you will ask a question and they will use the pointer to find the letter and name it. Have each student trace over the letter with his or her finger after correctly identifying and naming the letter. Ask the following questions:

   * Which letter is made with a line? (*Accept appropriate responses.*)
   * Which letter is made with a curve? (*Accept appropriate responses.*)
   * Which letter is made with a circle? (*Accept appropriate responses.*)
   * Which letter is made with a tail? (*Accept appropriate responses.*)

   Discuss the responses. Talk about how the letters of the alphabet are different and alike.

4. Distribute copies of the "Letters of the Alphabet" handouts and a set of crayons. Display the "Letters of the Alphabet" handouts on the chart stand. Name each picture and read each picture word aloud as the students read along silently.

5. Explain to the students that they will practice writing each letter of the alphabet in uppercase and lowercase. Direct their attention to the box with the picture of the octopus (page 141). Model writing an uppercase "O" and a lowercase "o" on the lines in the upper section of the box on the handout. Tell the students to do the same on their copy of the handout. Have them complete the handout by writing each uppercase and lowercase letter of the alphabet. Then, have the students connect the dashed lines to complete the picture in each box. Students can then color the pictures.

7. In a whole-group setting, ask volunteers to come up to the chart stand and write the uppercase and lowercase letters in each box. Discuss the correct formation of each letter.

Wrap-Up

* To conclude this lesson, have the students respond orally to the following question: *Why is it important to name, identify, and write the letters of the alphabet in uppercase and lowercase?*
* Ask volunteers to share their responses to the class. Discuss their responses for accuracy.

Uppercase and Lowercase Letters *(cont.)*

Uppercase and Lowercase Letters *(cont.)*

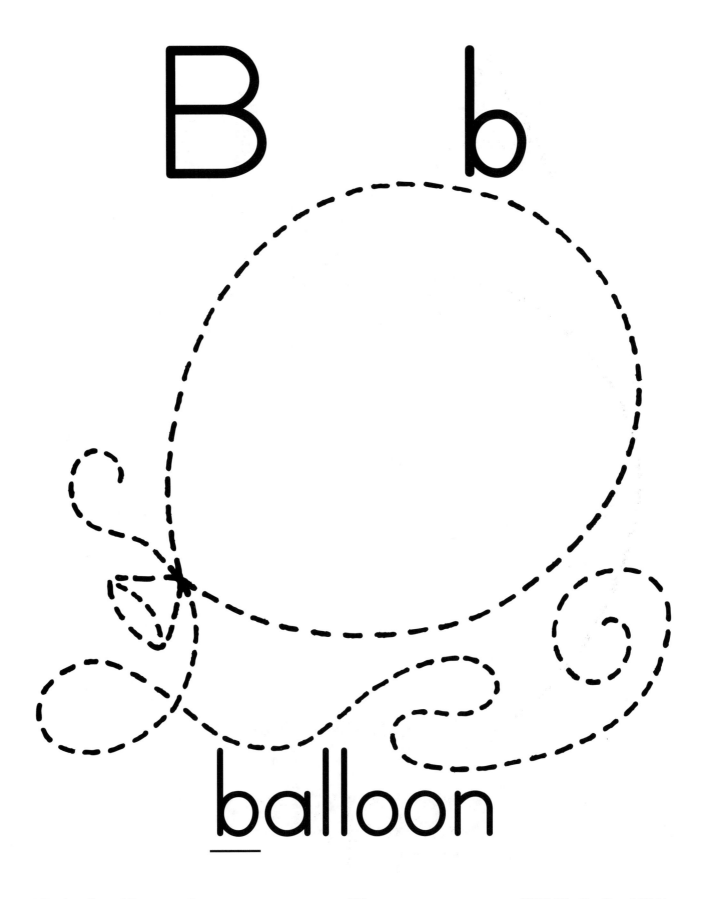

Uppercase and Lowercase Letters (cont.)

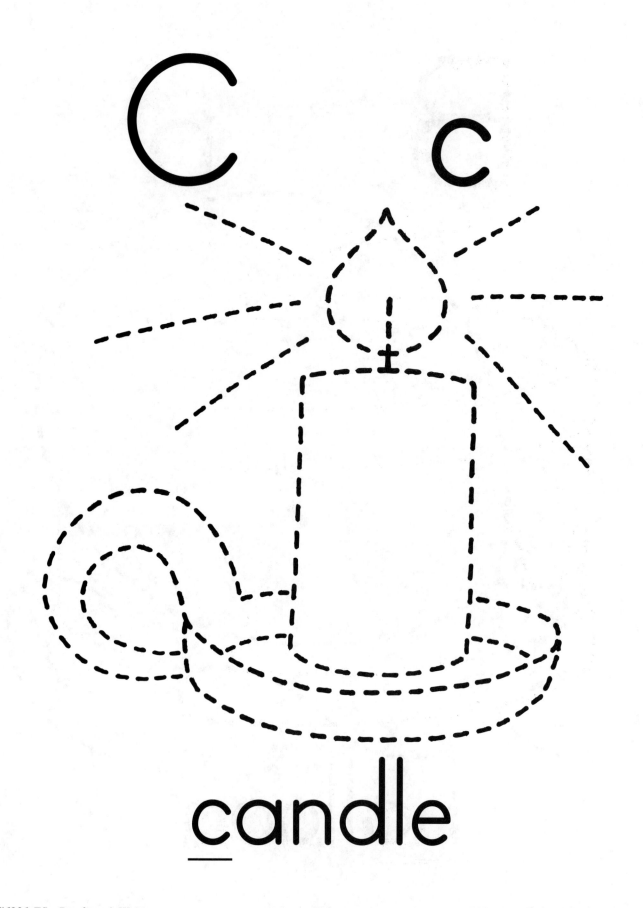

candle

Uppercase and Lowercase Letters (cont.)

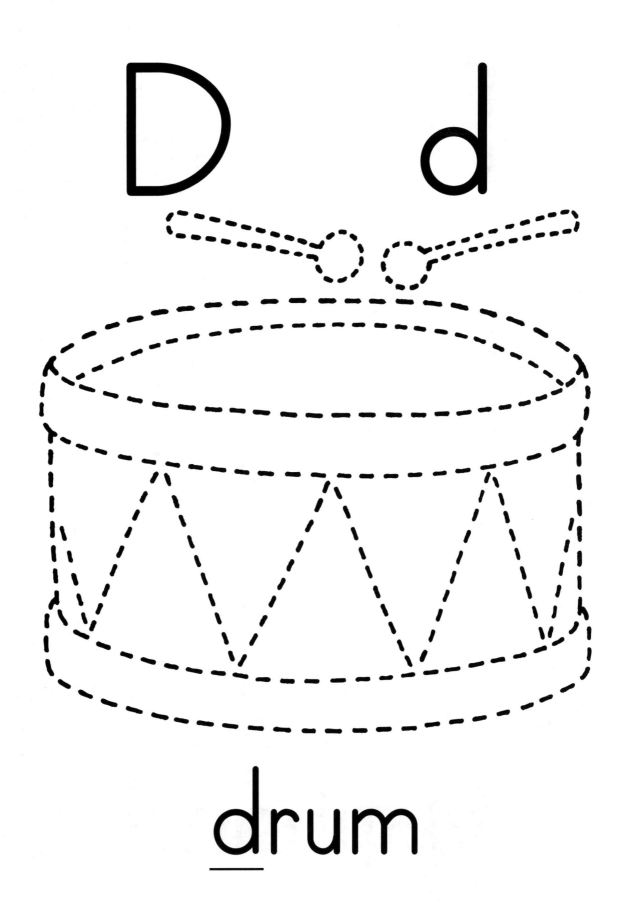

D d

drum

Uppercase and Lowercase Letters (cont.)

E e

elephant

Uppercase and Lowercase Letters (cont.)

F f

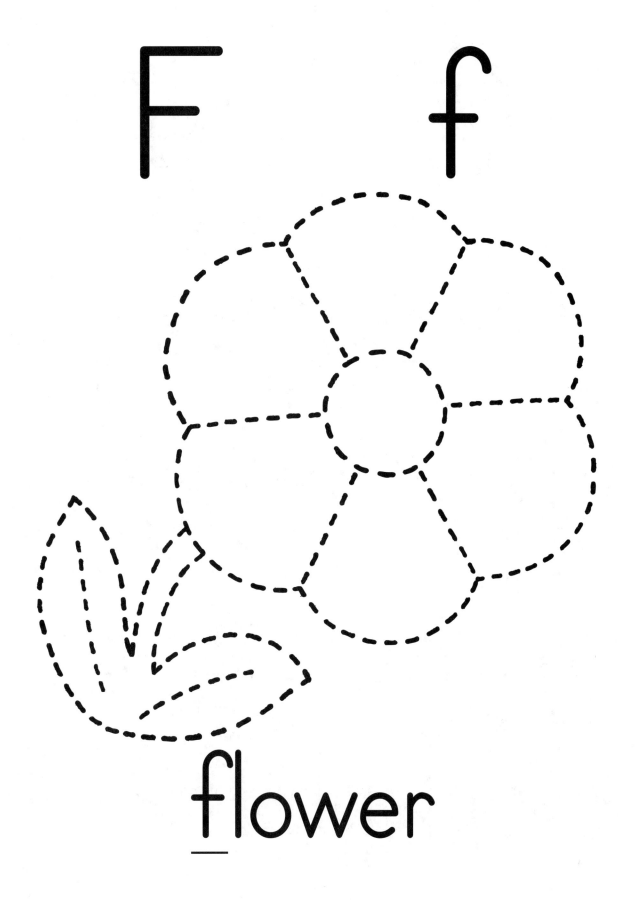

flower

Uppercase and Lowercase Letters *(cont.)*

G g

goat

Uppercase and Lowercase Letters (cont.)

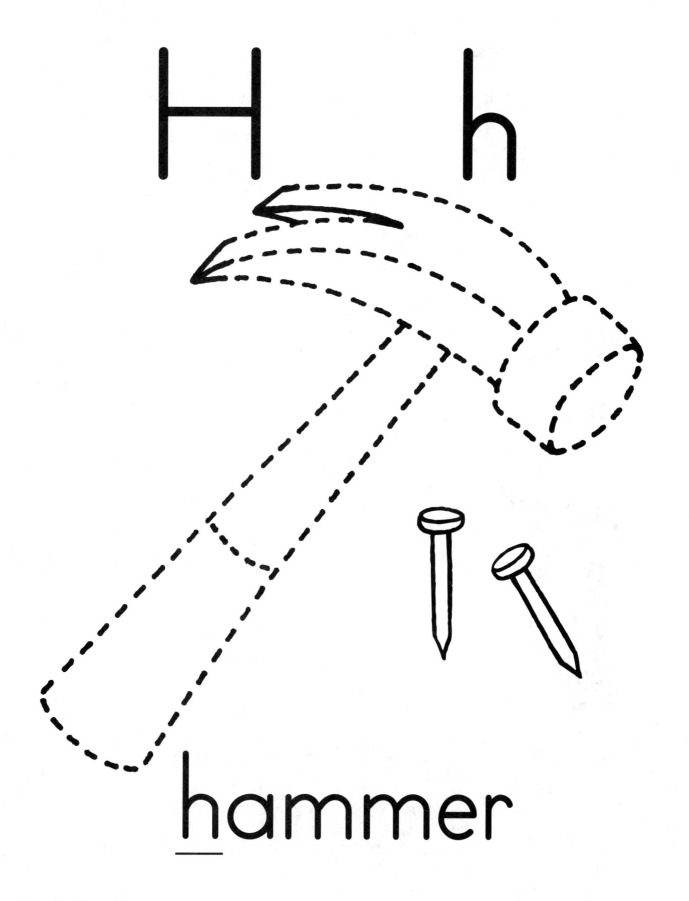

H h

hammer

Uppercase and Lowercase Letters *(cont.)*

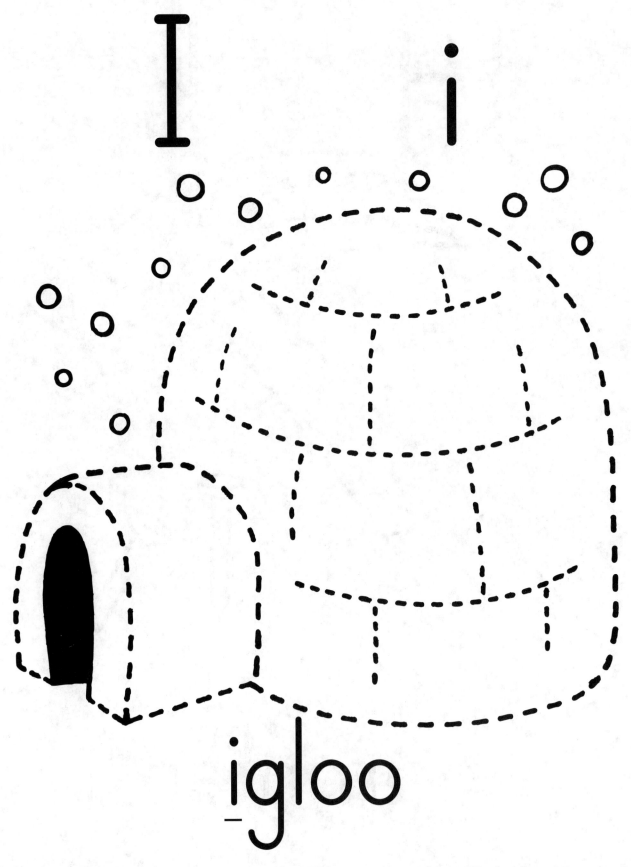

Uppercase and Lowercase Letters (cont.)

J j

jewels

Uppercase and Lowercase Letters *(cont.)*

K   k

key

Uppercase and Lowercase Letters *(cont.)*

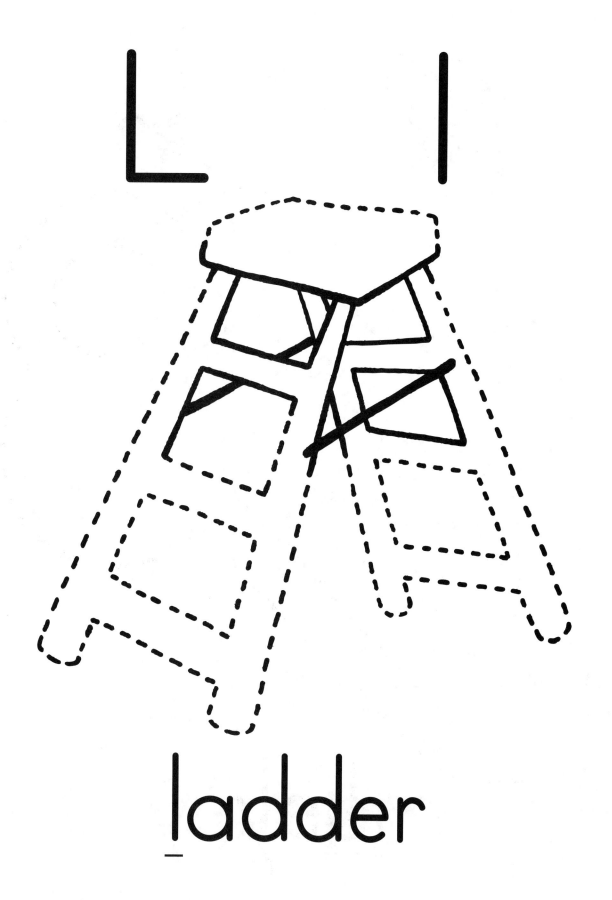

L l

ladder

Uppercase and Lowercase Letters *(cont.)*

M m

monkey

Uppercase and Lowercase Letters (cont.)

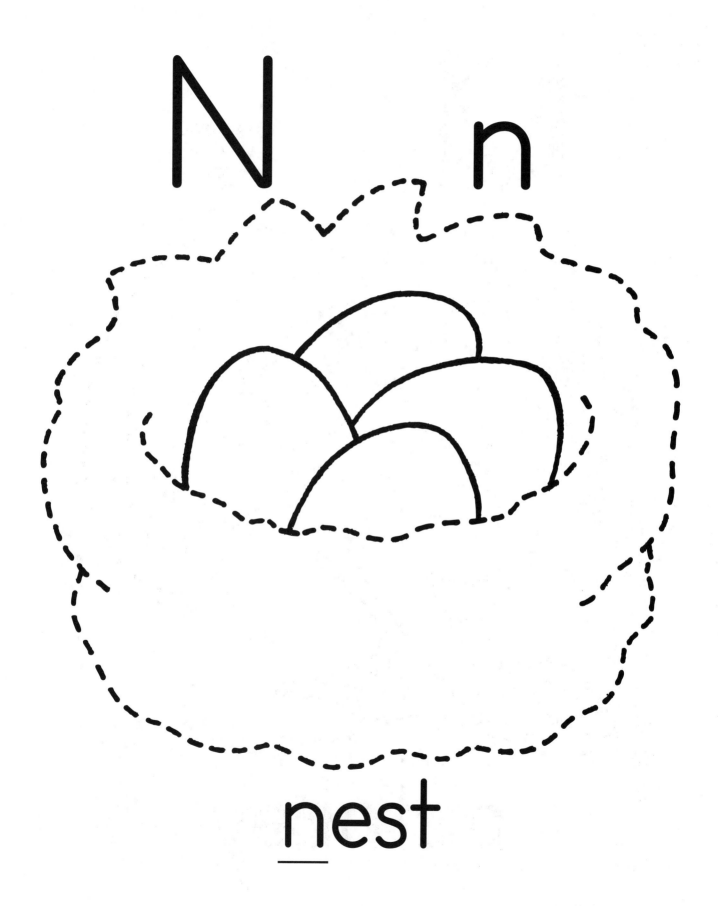

N n

nest

Uppercase and Lowercase Letters (cont.)

octopus

Uppercase and Lowercase Letters *(cont.)*

P p

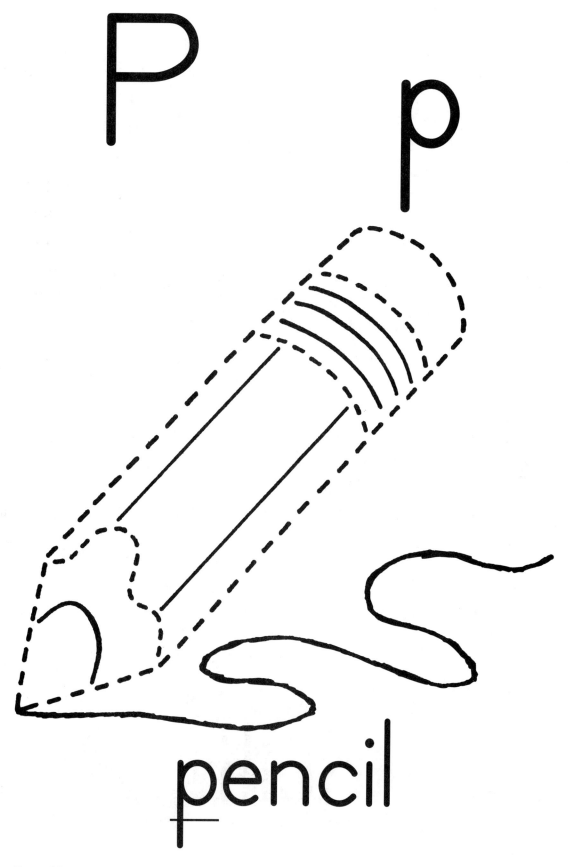

pencil

Uppercase and Lowercase Letters (cont.)

Q q

quilt

Uppercase and Lowercase Letters *(cont.)*

R r

ring

Uppercase and Lowercase Letters (cont.)

S s

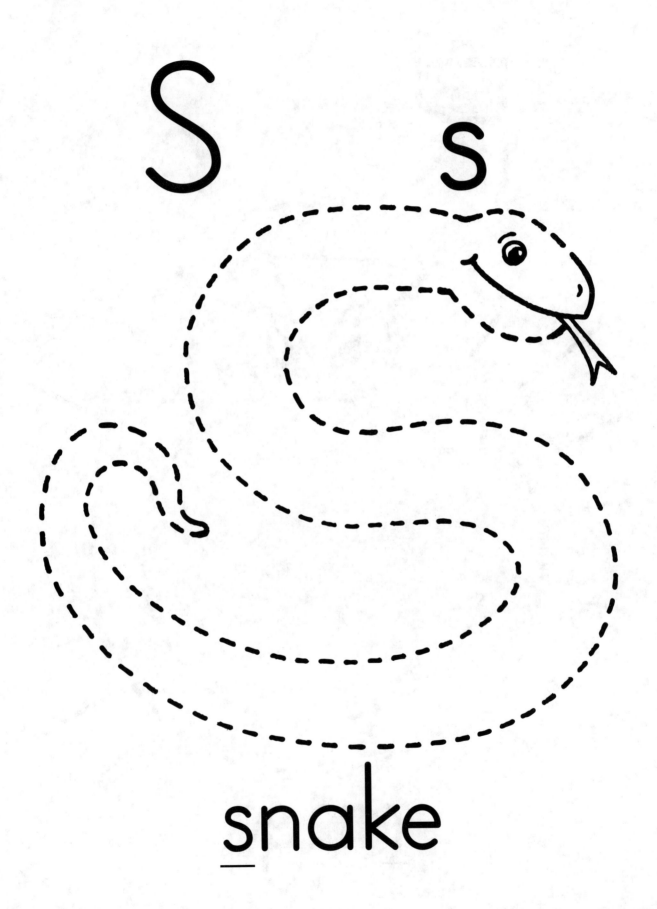

snake

Uppercase and Lowercase Letters *(cont.)*

Uppercase and Lowercase Letters *(cont.)*

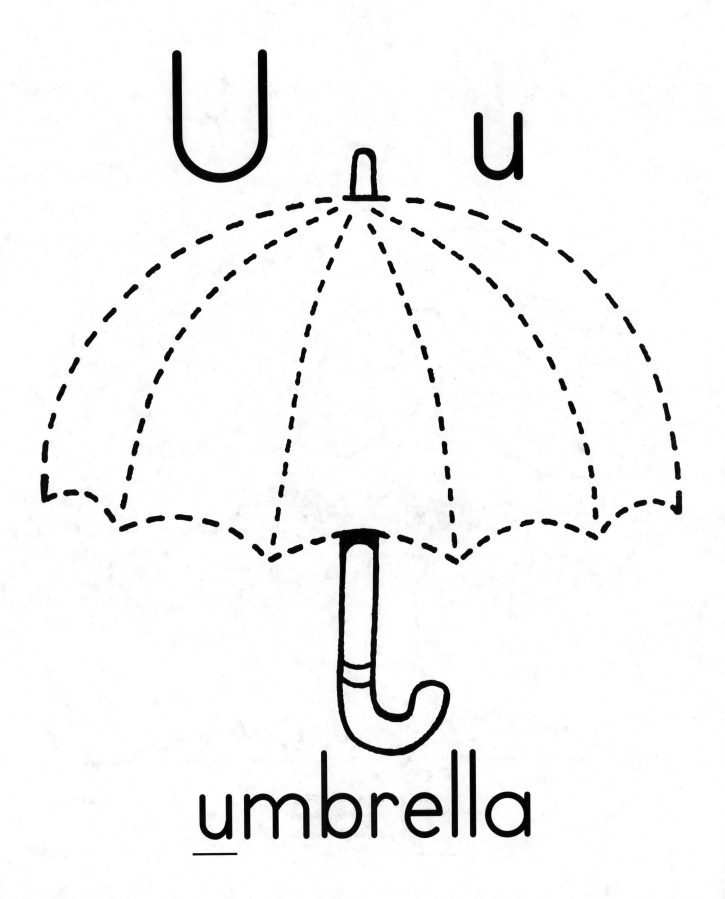

Uppercase and Lowercase Letters *(cont.)*

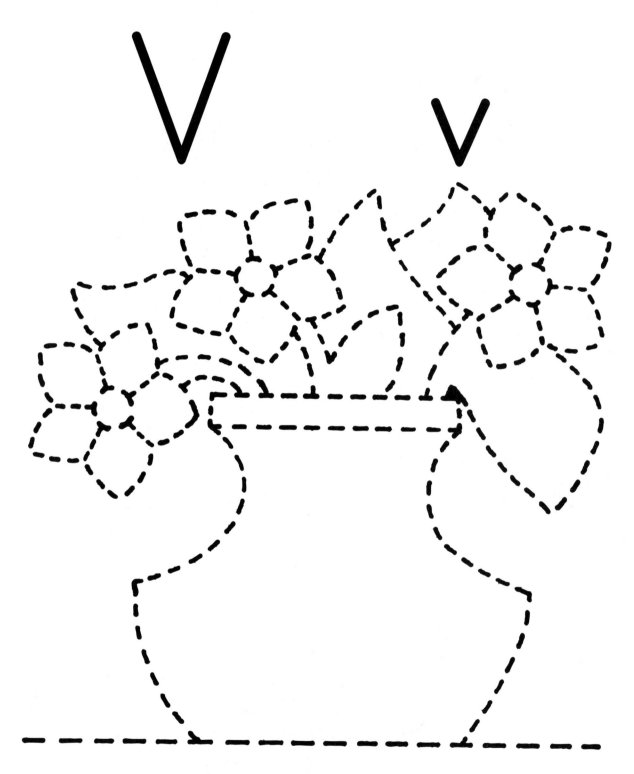

Uppercase and Lowercase Letters (cont.)

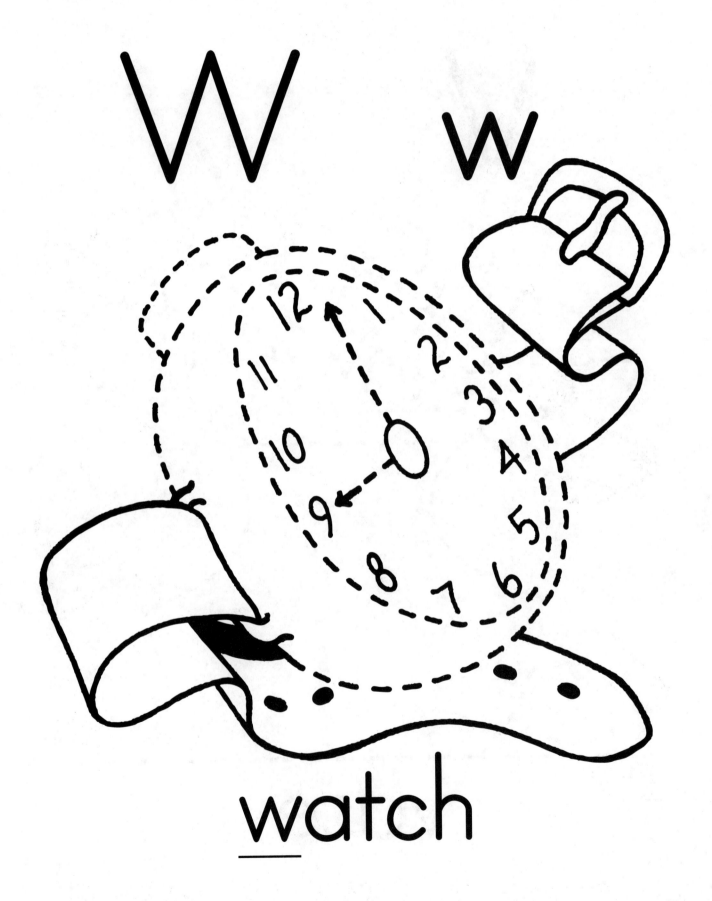

Uppercase and Lowercase Letters (cont.)

Uppercase and Lowercase Letters *(cont.)*

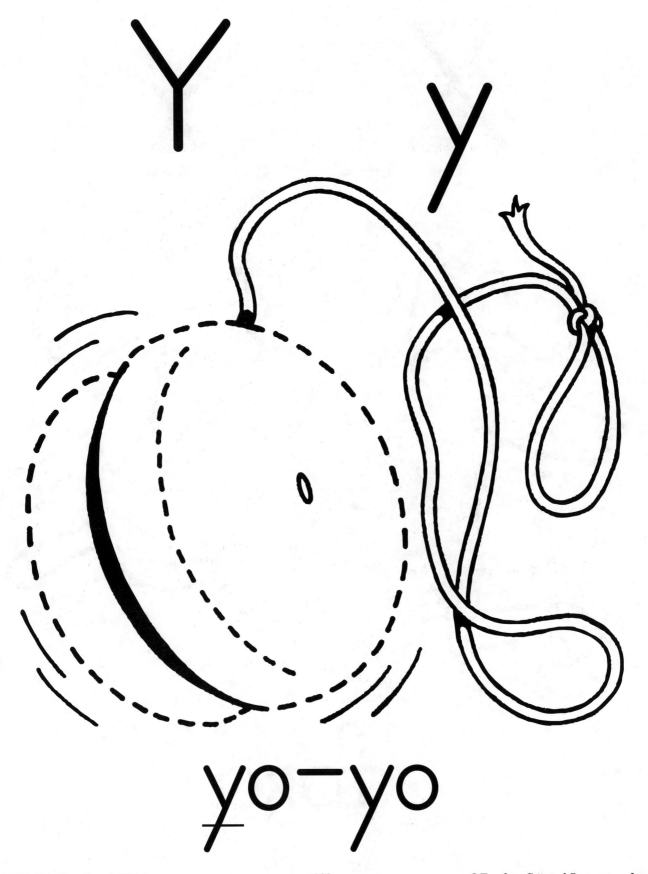

Uppercase and Lowercase Letters *(cont.)*

Z z

zebra

Name: _____

Uppercase and Lowercase Letters *(cont.)*

Letters of the Alphabet

Alphabet	_____ apple	_____ balloon
_____ candle	_____ drum	_____ elephant
_____ flower	_____ goat	_____ hammer

Uppercase and Lowercase Letters *(cont.)*

Letters of the Alphabet *(cont.)*

igloo	jewels	key
ladder	monkey	nest
octopus	pencil	quilt

Name: _____

Uppercase and Lowercase Letters *(cont.)*

Letters of the Alphabet *(cont.)*

___ ___ ring	___ ___ snake	___ ___ tree
___ ___ umbrella	___ ___ vase	___ ___ watch
___ ___ fox	___ ___ yo-yo	___ ___ zebra

#6221 ES: Reading & Writing   142   ©Teacher Created Resources, Inc.

Capitalization and Punctuation

Skill 22: The student will recognize how readers use capitalization and punctuation to comprehend.

Instructional Preparation

Choose or prepare the following:

- write a personal letter to the students explaining what they will learn today (*e.g., "Dear Class, Today we will be learning about capitals and punctuation. . . ."*)

Duplicate the following (one per student, unless otherwise indicated):

- "A Friendly Letter" handout
- "Capitals and Punctuation" handout

Prepare a transparency for the following:

- the prepared letter
- "A Friendly Letter" handout
- "Capitals and Punctuation" handout

Recall

Before beginning the **Review** component, display the transparency of the personal letter to the students. Read the letter aloud as the students follow along silently. (*Show excitement after exclamation points, and pause after commas and other punctuation to emphasize the punctuation marks.*) Facilitate a discussion based on the following questions:

- ✱ If the capitals and punctuation were removed from this letter, how would that change the letter? (*It would be harder to understand the letter.*)

- ✱ Why do writers capitalize words? (*So the reader knows where the sentences begin and recognizes which words are important.*)

- ✱ Why do writers use periods, question marks, exclamation points, and commas? (*So the reader can understand where the writer is starting and ending a thought; the writer is telling the reader something; the writer is asking something; the writer is excited about something; the writer needs the reader to pause while he or she reads.*)

Discuss student responses, focusing on the importance of using capitals and punctuation.

Review

1. Display a transparency of the "A Friendly Letter" handout, but cover the title and picture so the students are focusing on the displayed words only. Read the letter aloud as the students follow along silently. (*Read the words without stopping, pausing, or breaking for punctuation. Emphasize each word, but do not allow words to form complete thoughts.*) Ask the following questions (below and on page 144):

   - ✱ How do you know what this letter is about? (*You could go back and read some of the words to know a little about the letter, but it is hard to know what it is about.*)

©Teacher Created Resources, Inc.

Capitalization and Punctuation (cont.)

Review (cont.)

* Why is the letter difficult to understand? (*because the punctuation marks are missing, the reader does not know where one sentence ends and another begins*)

Facilitate a discussion, emphasizing the importance of using the words in the letter as clues to see where one sentence ends and another begins. Explain that this will help the reader know where the punctuation should be.

2. Put the students in groups of three or four. Distribute copies of the "A Friendly Letter" handout and uncover the title and pictures on the transparency. Read the title to students. Explain to the students that the handout is written in the form of a letter. Read the first line of words aloud to the students again, then read the first three words, "dear miss muffet." Explain that this is the beginning of the friendly letter. Underline each of the first letters in "dear miss muffet." Explain that each of these words needs to begin with a capital letter. Put a circle after the word "muffet." Explain that this is the end of a thought and a punctuation mark needs to be placed after that word. Model putting circles after the words that end each of the next three sentences and underlining the first letter of each word that needs to be capitalized. Explain to the students that they will be working in groups to figure out where punctuation and capitalization is needed. Allow time for the students to complete the letter.

3. Ask for volunteers to share their findings. Go through the letter with them, and discuss their responses for accuracy.

4. Distribute copies of the "Capitals and Punctuation" handout and display the transparency. Explain to the students that they will be writing the correct punctuation marks and capitals on their handout. Direct their attention to the box with the punctuation marks for a reference. Model for the students the correct way to start the letter, using capitals and punctuation marks. Do this for the first two sentences. Show them that they must look back at the letter to see where the breaks are for the sentences and to know which words must be capitalized. Have the students complete the handout on their own.

5. Ask for volunteers to share their changes with the class. Discuss their responses for accuracy.

6. Read the new letter while the students follow along. (Show excitement after the exclamation point, and pause after commas and other punctuation to emphasize the changes in the reading pattern from the previous reading without the proper punctuation.)

Wrap-Up

* To conclude this lesson, have the students respond orally to the following question: *How is capitalization and punctuation used to help readers understand what they read?*

* Ask volunteers to share their responses with the class. Discuss their responses for accuracy.

Capitalization and Punctuation (cont.)

A Friendly Letter

dear miss muffet hello i would like to introduce myself my name is mr small spider i like to climb up water spouts and live in houses when the sun comes up i spin webs i am so sorry i scared you i did not mean to make you run away i wanted to sit beside you will you please come back so we can talk your friend mr small spider

Capitalization and Punctuation (cont.)

Capitals and Punctuation

Directions: Place capitals on the lines. Place punctuation marks in the boxes.

period (.)	exclamation point (!)
question mark (?)	comma (,)

_____ ear _____ iss _____ uffet □

_____ ello □ _____ would like to introduce myself □

_____ y name is _____ r □ _____ mall _____ pider □

_____ like to climb up water spouts and live in houses □

_____ hen the sun comes up □ _____ spin webs □

_____ am so sorry _____ scared you □

_____ did not mean to make you run away □

_____ wanted to sit beside you □

_____ ill you please come back so we can talk □

_____ our friend □

_____ r □ _____ mall _____ pider

Sentence Patterns

Skill 23: The student will use a variety of sentence patterns such as interrogative requests and sentence fragments that convey emotion.

Instructional Preparation

Duplicate the following (one per student, unless otherwise indicated):

- "The Way Things Are Written" reference sheet
- "The Big Oak Tree" story
- "Writing Different Sentence Patterns" handout

Prepare a transparency of the following:

- "The Conversation" sheet
- "The Way Things Are Written" reference sheet
- "The Big Oak Tree" story
- "Writing Different Sentence Patterns" handout

Recall

Before beginning the **Review** component, display "The Conversation" transparency and read it aloud as the students read along silently. Give the students time to study the sentences. Facilitate a discussion based on the following questions:

- ✳ Which is an example of someone asking for something? (*"Will you go with me?"*)
- ✳ Which is an example of someone showing feelings? (*"What fun!"*)
- ✳ Which is an example of someone telling something? (*An appropriate response is as follows: "I am going to the store."*)

Review

1. Distribute copies of "The Way Things Are Written" reference sheet and display the transparency. Read each section aloud as the students read them silently. Discuss each section, using the examples provided to assist the students in their understanding. Ask the following questions:

   - ✳ What different sentence patterns do writers use? (*ones that ask for things; ones that show emotions or feelings; ones that tell something*)
   - ✳ What is an example of a sentence pattern that asks for something? (*Responses will vary; accept all reasonable responses.*)
   - ✳ What is an example of a sentence pattern that shows emotions or feelings? (*Responses will vary; accept all reasonable responses.*)
   - ✳ What is an example of a sentence pattern that tells something? (*Responses will vary; accept all reasonable responses.*)

Sentence Patterns (cont.)

Review (cont.)

2. Discuss the responses. Use the responses to point out that sentence patterns that ask questions end with a question mark, those that are written with strong emotion or feeling often end with an exclamation mark, and those that tell something end with a period.

3. Distribute copies of "The Big Oak Tree" story and display the transparency. Read the story aloud as the students read it silently. Ask the following questions:

   * What is the first sentence from the story that asks for something? (*"Who will help me find a new home?"*)

   * How do you know? (*because the sentence ends with a question mark and Owl is asking for help*)

4. Underline the asking sentence. Then continue using this same questioning style with the story to model and guide the students to find a sentence that is written with emotions or feelings and a sentence that tells something. Put a rectangle around the emotion sentence and a circle around the telling sentence. Have the students do the same on their copy of the story.

5. Put the students in pairs. Have the pairs work together to identify two more examples of each of the three types of sentence patterns in the story. Explain that they will need to underline the sentences that ask for something, put a rectangle around the sentences that show emotions or feelings, and circle the sentences that tell something.

6. When the students have completed this task, ask volunteers to share their responses. Discuss the responses for accuracy, recording several on the transparency.

7. Distribute copies of the "Writing Different Sentence Patterns" handout and display the transparency. Read the directions aloud as the students read them silently. Guide the students in completing the first two organizers. Then have them work independently to complete the rest of the handout. Circulate around the room during this activity and assist students as needed.

8. When the students have completed this task, ask for volunteers to share their responses. Discuss the responses for accuracy and write appropriate responses in the last two organizers. Use the responses to review how the different sentence patterns are used.

Wrap-Up

• To conclude the lesson, ask the following question: *How does a writer use sentence patterns to say things to the reader?*

• Allow time for the students to think about the answer. Discuss the responses. Emphasize the different ways that writers use sentence patterns: to ask for things, to show feelings or emotions, or to tell things.

Sentence Patterns (cont.)

The Conversation

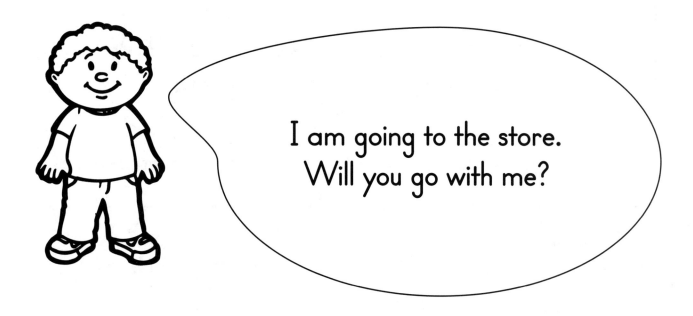

I am going to the store.
Will you go with me?

What fun! Yes, I will!

Sentence Patterns (cont.)

The Way Things Are Written

Writers use different sentence patterns to say things.

Writers can ask for things — (?)
- Can you go with me?
- Will you help me?
- Who will help me?

Writers can show emotions or feelings — (!)
- No way!
- Me too!
- Me first!

Writers can tell things — (.)
- The boy has blue shoes.
- The truck stopped three times.
- Today, she will go fishing.

Sentence Patterns (cont.)

The Big Oak Tree
adapted from the folktale "The Little Red Hen"

The red barn was home to four animal friends. Owl, Squirrel, Rabbit, and Mouse lived there. Owl knew the barn was very old. He knew they would need another home soon. He wanted to look for a new home. He asked his friends to help.

"Who will help me find a new home?"

"Not me!" said Squirrel.

"No way!" said Rabbit.

"I'm busy!" said Mouse.

Owl found a big oak tree all by himself. He wanted to clean the new home. He asked his friends to help.

"Who will help me clean the new home?"

"Not me!" said Squirrel.

"No way!" said Rabbit.

"I'm busy!" said Mouse.

It took Owl all week to clean the new home. When Owl was done, the old red barn started to fall. He asked his friends one last time. "Who will help me live in the new home?"

"I will!" said Squirrel.

"Me too!" said Rabbit.

"Count me in!" said Mouse.

Owl told his friends to find their own home. He was the only one who looked for it. He was the only one who cleaned it.

He told them he would be the only one to live in the big oak tree. And that is just what he did.

Name: _____

Sentence Patterns *(cont.)*

Writing Different Sentence Patterns

Directions: Look at the animal pictured in each box. Then, in the spaces provided, write three sentences. Ask the animal a question for the first sentence. Write the animal's answer with a lot of feeling or emotion for the second sentence. Write a sentence that tells something for the third sentence.

Question (?): _____

Answer (!): _____

Tell Something: _____

Question (?): _____

Answer (!): _____

Tell Something: _____

Question (?): _____

Answer (!): _____

Tell Something: _____

Question (?): _____

Answer (!): _____

Tell Something: _____

#6221 ES: Reading & Writing © Teacher Created Resources, Inc.

Using Graphic Organizers

Skill 24: The student will use charts, webs, illustrations, and story maps to summarize information from a passage.

Instructional Preparation

Materials:

- large color photographs of a koala and a platypus

Duplicate the following (one per student, unless otherwise indicated):

- "They're Not Really Bears" passage
- "Using Charts" reference sheet
- "Using Webs" reference sheet
- "It's Not a Duck" passage
- "Platypus Facts" handouts

Prepare a transparency of the following:

- "They're Not Really Bears" passage
- "Using Charts" reference sheet
- "Using Webs" reference sheet
- "It's Not a Duck" passage
- "Platypus Facts" handouts

Recall

Before beginning the **Review** component, facilitate a discussion based on this question:

❋ What is a chart? (*information given in the form of a table, graph, or diagram*)

Review

1. To begin the lesson, write on the classroom board the following three colors: *blue*, *purple*, and *red*. Ask the students to choose their favorite color given the choice of these three colors. Have the students who chose the color blue as their favorite color stand up. Create and complete a concept web on the left side of the classroom board, in which the center oval is labeled "Blue" and the extensions from the center oval contain the names of the students in the class who chose blue as their favorite color. Repeat this procedure with the colors purple and red, with the web for purple created on the middle section of the board and the web for red on the right side. Discuss how each of the webs summarizes, or reviews, the information about the students' favorite color given three choices of color.

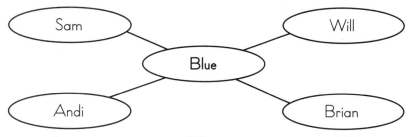

Using Graphic Organizers (cont.)

Review (cont.)

2. Tell the students you are going to show them another organizer that can help summarize the information about the students' favorite color given three choices of color. Create and complete on a sheet of chart paper a three-column chart entitled "Favorite Color" with the first column labeled "Blue," the second labeled "Purple," and the third labeled "Red." Write the names of the students in the appropriate columns based on the information provided in the step 1. Explain how using charts and webs is also an effective way to summarize information read in a passage. Tell the students that in this lesson they will read several passages and summarize the information in charts and webs.

3. Distribute copies of the "They're Not Really Bears" passage and display the transparency. If available, also display a large color photograph of a koala. Read the passage aloud while the students read along silently and then ask the following questions:

   * What is the passage mainly about? (*koalas*)

   * What kind of information does the passage give about koalas? (*where they live, what they eat, what they are like, how they care for their young, etc.*)

   When asking the second question, direct the students' attention to the headings in the passage. Explain how looking at the headings in a passage can help a reader more easily figure out the information in the passage.

   On the classroom board, create and complete a concept web with the center oval labeled "Koalas: They're Not Really Bears" and the extensions labeled with the headings in the passage. Tell the students that this is one way to summarize the information in a passage; however, it does not give specific information about koalas. (Note: Leave this web on the board as an example.)

4. Direct the students' attention back to the "They're Not Really Bears" passage and ask a volunteer to reread the first section, or paragraph, of the passage while the rest of the students read along silently. Then ask the following question:

   * Where do koalas live? (*in Australia, in forests, mostly in trees, etc.*)

   Discuss the responses, referring to the first four sentences of the passage's first paragraph and underlining this information, if necessary, to help student understanding. Tell the students that they are going to use a chart to summarize the information about where koalas live.

Using Graphic Organizers *(cont.)*

Review *(cont.)*

5. Distribute copies of the "Using Charts" handout and display the transparency. Read the directions aloud as the students read them silently. Direct the students' attention to the first chart titled "Things About Koalas" and the first column of the chart labeled "Where Koalas Live." Show the students how one of the responses to the question, "in forests," is already written in the chart for them, then model how to complete the first column of the chart by writing the other two responses—"in Australia" and "mostly in trees"—in the two empty boxes in this column. Have the students do the same on their copies of the handout.

6. Redisplay the "They're Not Really Bears" transparency and ask a volunteer to reread the second section, or paragraph, of the passage while the rest of the students read along silently. Then ask the following question:

    ✳ What are koalas? *(They are not bears; they are mammals; they are part of a group called marsupials.)*

    Discuss the responses and redisplay the "Using Charts" transparency. With the students' assistance, complete the second column of the "Things About Koalas" chart on the transparency while the students complete it on their copy of the handout. The final chart should look like this:

Things About Koalas

Where Koalas Live	What Koalas Are
in Australia	are not bears
in forests	are mammals
mostly in trees	are marsupials

7. Redisplay the "They're Not Really Bears" transparency and reread the third section (third and fourth paragraphs) of the passage aloud while the students read along silently. Show the students how to complete the second chart on the "Using Charts" handout titled "Koala Habits" by referring the students to the third paragraph of the passage to complete the first column of the chart and to the first paragraph to complete the second column of the chart. Here are the answers:

Koala Habits

Eating Leaves	Climbing Trees
eat at night	climb using claws
eat only eucalyptus leaves	hands have two thumbs
store leaves in cheeks	feet have ridged skin
eat over a pound of leaves a day	leap from treetop to treetop

Using Graphic Organizers (cont.)

Review (cont.)

8. Tell the students that they are now going to use webs to summarize the information in a passage. Distribute copies of the "Using Webs" handout and display the transparency. Discuss the information that is already provided on the web that supports what koalas are like, referring to these pieces of information in the third section of the "They're Not Really Bears" passage. Then work with the students to write in the important information about what koalas are like in the empty boxes on the web. Here is a sample of the completed web:

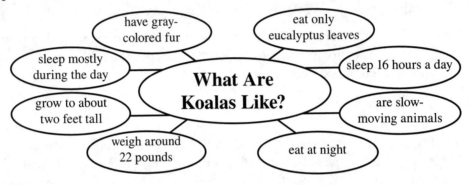

9. Have the students get in three-person groups. Distribute copies of the "It's Not a Duck" passage and display the transparency. If available, also display a large color photograph of a platypus. Read the passage aloud while the students read along silently. Ask the students what the passage is mainly about and what kind of information is in the passage.

10. Distributes copies of the "Platypus Facts" handout. Read the directions aloud as the students read them silently. Have the members of each group work together to complete the chart and the web. Have each member write the answers on his or her handout. Circulate around the room to provide assistance. If the students need help, let them know that the information for the chart can be found in the first paragraph and the information for the web can be found in the third paragraph. (As an extension of the activity, you could create a chart and/or web that prompts students to use the information contained in the second and/or fourth paragraphs, as well.)

What a Platypus Looks Like

Head	Body
soft and rubbery	flat tail
mouth shaped like duck's bill	covered in thick black fur
no teeth	
hidden ears	
small eyes	

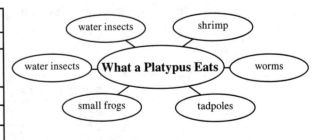

Wrap Up

- To conclude instruction, ask the following question: *How can you summarize a passage using charts and webs?*
- Ask volunteers to share their responses. Use the responses to review how to use charts and webs to summarize information from a passage.

They're Not Really Bears

Where Do They Live?

Koalas are found in Australia. They live in forests. They climb trees. They mostly live in trees. Koalas have claws. They grab onto the trees with their back legs and strong hands. Their hands have two thumbs. Their feet have ridged skin. This helps them climb trees. They can also leap from treetop to treetop.

What Are Koalas?

Koalas are not bears. Like bears, they are mammals. But they are part of a group called marsupials. Marsupials have pouches. The pouches are for their young. Kangaroos are also marsupials.

What Are They Like?

Koalas have gray-colored fur. It feels like the wool on a sheep. They can grow over two feet tall. They weigh around twenty-two pounds. Koalas sleep mostly during the day. At night, they eat leaves. Koalas only like to eat eucalyptus leaves. They can store these leaves in their cheeks. They eat over one pound of leaves a day.

Koalas are slow-moving animals. They need a lot of sleep. They sleep about 16 hours a day. They sometimes fall asleep when they are eating.

How Do They Care for Their Young?

Female koalas care for their babies for one year. When baby koalas are born, they are very small. They are about the size of a jellybean. They are born without fur. They live inside their mother's pouch. Soon they will grow too big for the pouch. Then they will climb onto their mother's back. After a year they are ready to be on their own. Then they will live alone in the trees just like their mother and father.

Using Graphic Organizers (cont.)

Using Charts

Directions: Complete each chart using the "They're Not Really Bears" passage.

Things About Koalas

Where Koalas Live	What Are Koalas
	are not bears
in forests	

Things About Koalas

Eating Leaves	Climbing Trees
eat at night	
	feet have ridged skin
	leap from treetop to treetop

Using Graphic Organizers (cont.)

Using Webs

Directions: Complete the web using the "They're Not Really Bears" passage.

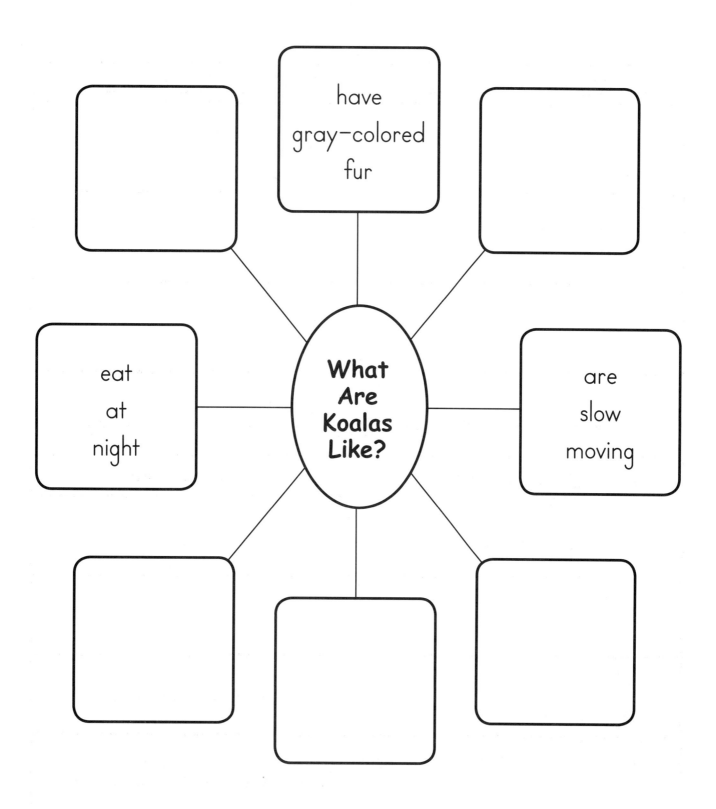

Using Graphic Organizers (cont.)

It's Not a Duck

It lays eggs. It has a duck's bill. It sure sounds like a duck. But it's not a duck. It is a platypus.

What Does It Look Like?

It is sometimes called a duckbilled platypus. It gets this name from its soft and rubbery mouth. Its mouth is shaped like a duck's bill. It has no teeth. It crushes its food using ridges inside its bill. It has ears that you cannot see. Its eyes are small. Its tail is flat like a beaver's tail. It is covered in a thick brown fur. It is about two feet long. Its tail is usually six inches long. It weighs about four pounds.

How Does It Move?

The platypus has webbed feet like a duck. Its feet have five toes. It is a good swimmer. The front feet help it swim. Its back feet and tail are used to steer when swimming. They are also used to stop.

The platypus moves well on land. It walks on its knuckles. It does this because of its webbed feet. It also has claws. The claws let it dig and climb trees.

What and How Does It Eat?

The platypus eats water insects, shrimp, worms, tadpoles, small frogs, and fish. It hunts in the water at night. It closes its eyes, ears, and nose underwater. Its sight and hearing are useless in the water at night. The platypus finds its food by feeling movement in the water. It stores its food in pouches in its cheek. Then it will take the food to the surface to eat it.

Where Does It Live?

The platypus is found in Australia. It lives along streams and lakes. It lives alone in a burrow. A burrow is a nest. It makes this along the banks of a river or lake. It was actually alive during the time of the dinosaurs!

Name: _____

Using Graphic Organizers (cont.)

Platypus Facts

What a Platypus Looks Like

Head	Body
soft and rubbery mouth shaped like a duck's bill	

What a Platypus Eats

- water insects

PAL Packets

Introduction

PAL Packets are an important component of the Essential Skills series. PAL stands for "Parent Assisted Learning," and each PAL Packet lesson is meant to supplement student learning with a short activity that gives parents and guardians the tools to help their children practice important skills.

The following lessons can be found in both English and Spanish on the CDs that accompany this book. A sample PAL lesson has been provided in both English and Spanish in the pages that follow.

Common Sight Words ✽ *Learn to recognize common sight words.*

Compound Words ✽ *Learn how to figure out the meaning of compound words.*

Decoding ✽ *Learn to figure out a picture that matches the last word of a sentence.*

Differentiate Letters, Words, and Sentences ✽ *Learn to identify and tell the difference between letters, words, and sentences.*

End Punctuation ✽ *Learn to use end punctuation.*

Letter-Sound Correspondence ✽ *Learn to make sense of words by matching letters to their sounds.*

Make Predictions ✽ *Learn to make predictions while reading a story.*

Modifiers ✽ *Learn to use modifiers (describing words) to add information and interest to a sentence.*

One-Step Directions ✽ *Learn to follow one-step directions.*

Organizational Strategies ✽ *Learn to plan writing by organizing ideas and information.*

Rhyming Words ✽ *Learn to create and state rhyming words.*

Sequence ✽ *Learn the order of events in a story.*

Unknown Word ✽ *Learn to identify unknown words and their meanings by using context clues and previous knowledge/experience with words.*

PAL PACKET

Parent Assisted Learning (PAL)

Reading/Language Arts
Grade 1
Decoding

PAL PACKET

Dear Parent or Guardian:

Your child is currently learning to figure out a picture that matches the last word of a sentence. He or she is to do this using decoding skills and meaning in context. Here is your chance to help your child practice this important skill.

In this PAL Packet you will find a short activity for you and your child to do. Please do the activity and "The Back Page." Then sign your name on "The Back Page" and have your child return it by _____.

Thanks for your help.

Sincerely,

_____

Decoding

Knowing the Last Word in a Sentence

Parent Pointer

Every word in a sentence is important. In order to understand what a sentence is expressing, a reader must know how to say every word and understand its meaning. To find out what a word is, a reader can do two things: sound out all of the letters in the word, then say the sounds together to make the word; or use the other words in the sentence to figure out what the word is. Using these two strategies will help your child better understand the words he or she reads and make your child a better reader. When your child can draw a picture that represents the last word in the sentence, then you will know that your child understands what has been read.

Student Directions

Have your child read the sentence in the first arrow on the "You Always Have the Last Word!" page to you. Then have him or her look at the last word. Have him or her draw a picture of the last word in the space provided. If your child cannot figure out the word, have him or her sound out each letter in the word. Then have him or her say all the sounds together to make the word. Tell your child to also use the other words in the sentence to figure out what the word is. Then have him or her read the rest of the sentences and draw a picture for the last word of each sentence. Tell him or her to draw the pictures in the spaces provided. Check each picture to make sure it matches the last word of the sentence.

Talk About It

After you have finished the activity, go to "The Back Page" to show what you know.

Now go have some fun with the activity!

Decoding

You Always Have the Last Word!

My first gift was a cute black-and-white puppy.

The room was decorated with red, white, and blue balloons.

Decoding

You Always Have the Last Word! *(cont.)*

> For a snack, my mom gave me milk and cookies.

> I tripped and fell hard into the thick, green grass.

Decoding

You Always Have the Last Word! *(cont.)*

> The house warmed up due to the hot midday sun.

> Beau went to the park to see the big parade.

Decoding

The Back Page

Talk About It

Parent ➤ Ask your son or daughter the following question:
- How can a reader figure out what the last word of a sentence is?

Student ➤ Answer the above question in complete sentences.

➤ **Do the following activity on a separate piece of paper:**
- Tell your child to find pictures of objects, things, or places in magazines or newspapers. Have him or her cut out the pictures and glue them on a separate sheet of paper. Tell your child to write the word that names the picture below each picture. Then have him or her write sentences using each of the words. The word that stands for the picture should be the last word in the sentence.

Student's Name _Parent or Guardian's Signature_

©Teacher Created Resources, Inc. #6221 ES: Reading & Writing

PAL PACKET

Parent Assisted Learning (PAL)

Lectura/Artes del lenguaje
Grado 1
Descifrando

PAL PACKET

Estimado padre/madre o tutor legal:

Actualmente su hijo/a está aprendiendo a entender un dibujo que coteja a la última palabra de una oración. Lo hará usando habilidades para descifrar y el significado en contexto.

Esta es su oportunidad para ayudarle a practicar esta importante habilidad.

En este paquete PAL encontrará una actividad corta para hacer junto con su hijo/a. Favor de hacer la actividad y "La última página". Después firme "La última página" y mándela con su hijo/a el día _____.

Gracias por su ayuda.

Atentamente,

_____

Descifrando

Saber la última palabra de una oración

Consejo para los padres

Cada palabra en una oración es importante. Para comprender lo que una oración expresa, un lector debe saber cómo decir cada palabra y comprender su significado. Para saber lo que significa una palabra, un lector puede hacer dos cosas: pronunciar cada letra de la palabra y luego pronunciar los sonidos juntos para formar la palabra; o usar las otras palabras en la oración para averiguar el significado. Usar estas dos estrategias le ayudará a su hijo/a comprender mejor las palabras que lea y le ayudará a ser un mejor lector. Cuando su hijo/a pueda hacer un dibujo que representa el significado de la última palabra de la oración, usted sabrá que su hijo/a entiende lo que se ha leído.

Instrucciones para el estudiante

Pídale a su hijo/a que le lea la oración de la primera flecha de la página "¡Siempre tiene la última palabra!". Después, pídale que vea la última palabra. Pídale que haga un dibujo de la última palabra en el espacio provisto. Si su hijo/a no puede averiguar el significado de la palabra, pídale que pronuncie cada letra de la palabra. Luego, pídale que pronuncie todos los sonidos juntos para formar la palabra. Dígale a su hijo/a que use también las otras palabras de la oración para descifrar el significado. Pídale que lea las otras oraciones y que haga un dibujo del significado de la última palabra de cada oración. Dígale que haga los dibujos en los espacios provistos. Revise cada dibujo para ver si se relaciona con el significado.

Hablen sobre la actividad

Después de terminar la actividad, pasen a "La última página" para que su hijo/a muestre lo que sabe.

¡Ahora diviértanse con la actividad!

Descifrando

¡Siempre tiene la última palabra!

Mi primer regalo fue un lindo perrito.

El cuarto estaba decorado con muchos globos.

Descifrando

¡Siempre tiene la última palabra! *(continuación)*

Como merienda, mi mamá me dio leche y galletas.

Me tropecé y me caí fuertemente sobre el pasto verde y grueso.

Descifrando

¡Siempre tiene la última palabra! *(continuación)*

La casa se calentó debido al sol.

Benito fue al parque para ver el desfile.

Descifrando

La última página

Hablen sobre la actividad

Padre/madre ➜ Haga a su hijo/a la siguiente pregunta:
- ¿Cómo un lector puede descifrar el significado de la última palabra de una oración?

Estudiante ➜ Conteste las pregunta anteriores con oraciones completas en el espacio que sigue.

_____
_____
_____
_____
_____
_____

➜ **Haga la siguiente actividad en una hoja de papel:**
- Dígale a su hijo/a que encuentre fotos de objetos, cosas o lugares en revistas y periódicos. Pídale que recorte las fotos y las pegue a una hoja de papel. Dígale a su hijo/a que escriba la palabra que nombra la foto debajo de cada una. Después, pídale que escriba oraciones usando cada una de las palabras. La palabra que describe la foto deberá ser la última palabra en la oración.

_____   _____
Nombre del estudiante   Firma del padre/madre o tutor legal